The BRIMPTS TIN MINES Dartmeet

ROGER BIRD
and
PETER HIRST

Number 1 in a series of reports by the
DARTMOOR TINWORKING RESEARCH GROUP

DTRG

Contents

Figures

First published in Great Britain in 1996
by the Dartmoor Tinworking Research Group
c/o 3 Tappers Close, Topsham, Exeter, Devon EX3 0DG

ISBN 0 9529442 0 0

Printed by:-
Peter Howell & Co., The Printing Press, 21 Clare Place, Coxside, Plymouth PL4 0JW

Acknowledgements

We would like to thank all those people and organisations who helped us research the history of the Brimpts Mines, who granted access or gave practical help. In particular, the Bradford family at Brimpts for access and help, the Forestry Commission who supplied the posts for the visitor trail and helped with clearance in the plantation and, from the DTRG, Dr Tom Greeves who supplied some vital references and gave useful guidance, Phil Newman who taught us surveying techniques, Elaine and John Viant who helped clear much of the debris around the dressing floors and assisted with detailed surveying, Mike Brown for information on timber purchases, and Hélène and Ted Fitch. The Duchy of Cornwall and Dartmoor National Park Authority were consulted and gave guidance in respect of the visitor trail. We are also grateful to the Dartmoor National Park Authority for a grant towards publication costs.

In telling the history of the mines, the authors have, of necessity, had to compile a story from very incomplete data and whilst we believe that the text is as accurate as possible, it should be borne in mind that it is our interpretation and not all detail may be correct. If any readers have further information on the mines which can supplement our data we would welcome details sent to the address below.

Dartmoor Tinworking Research Group

If you have an interest in tinworking in and around Dartmoor, you may like to join DTRG, the Dartmoor Tinworking Research Group. This was formed in 1991 to encourage field and documentary research into the tin industry and to promote public awareness and appreciation of its effects on Devon life. Besides receiving a regular newsletter, guided walks and talks, members can receive training and gain practical experience through projects such as the major survey of tinworking in the Walkham Valley which includes excavation of the Upper Merrivale Tin Mills. For further details, please contact the Membership Secretary:- Peter Hirst, Badger's Holt Bungalow, Dartmeet, Princetown, Yelverton, Devon PL20 6SG. Telephone or Fax. 01364 631550

Introduction

The visitor to the Southwest will probably be aware of Cornwall's long mining history if only because of the old engine houses that conjure up the sort of rugged, romantic image not usually associated with industrial dereliction. Dartmoor too has an equally long mining history and even a few engine houses, but nearly all of the workings relied on water for their power source and the remains are far less obvious. Tin was sought in the middle of the moor; tin, copper, lead, silver and other minerals on the edges. Initially water was used to separate cassiterite, the dense tin ore, from granite waste in tin 'streaming' operations in valley bottoms where the ore had accumulated. The recovered ore, 'black tin', was smelted with wood or peat charcoal in furnaces which, from about 1300 onwards, were in 'blowing houses'; mills where the blast for the furnace was provided by bellows powered by a waterwheel.

As reserves of stream tin began to run out, the tinners turned their efforts to mining cassiterite from the mineral veins or 'lodes' in the granite. This was shallow surface mining in the excavations we now call openworks. The tin ore from these was bound up in the rocks of the lode and the stones had to be crushed to release it, leading to the development of 'knacking' or stamping mills where iron-shod wooden baulks were raised by teeth on an axle driven by a waterwheel and then let fall onto the rocks.

Finally, as these shallow deposits also were worked out, underground mining took over. The problem of flooding was overcome initially using drainage by gravity down adits, near-horizontal tunnels driven through the hillside from a valley to the bottom of the mine. Only when efficient pumps were developed, again waterwheel-powered, was deep mining viable. There was however one major problem, the near-vertical lodes were generally narrow, the rock hard to mine and the tin content small, a recipe as we shall see for economic disaster.

Attracted by the history of earlier rich pickings from the streaming and openworks and buoyed by the success of mines in Cornwall, in the Tamar Valley and the rare profitable Dartmoor mine, 19th century investors sank their money in many small tin mines that popped up wherever a tin-bearing lode could be found. Brimpts was one such site.

Situated adjacent to Dartmeet in the east central part of Dartmoor, Brimpts was one of the inner ring of mines surrounding the high northern moor. Its history is a long and interesting one. Early tin streaming is not clearly represented (although there are suggestions in places), but there are openworks and three underground mines. The map in Fig. 1. shows a plan of the layout of the Brimpts mining area or 'sett'. It was claimed as the area bounded by the East and West Dart Rivers and Bellever Tor, but more realistically, the area from Laughter Tor through to the East Dart River east of Brimpts Farm was the prime objective and within this, the sites of North Mine and South Mine (which included the gully and the plantation) were the principal workings.

Until recently, little had been written about these mines and they had sunk into obscurity, but the two authors, in the course of researching the documented history and surveying the workings have found a history that seems to be worth telling because it is typical of events at so many of these small mines. We hope you will enjoy reading it.

If, having done so, you wish to visit the Brimpts Mines, a visitor trail has been set up starting from Brimpts Farm. Please be aware though that the gully and the route to the plantation above Brimpts are on private land and access to these areas is a privilege accorded to customers of Brimpts' catering and purchasers of this report or trail guide (available from Brimpts Farm). Please leave gates as you find them.

Note: A fold-out plan of the three main workings is at the end of the report. You will probably need to refer to this as you read on.

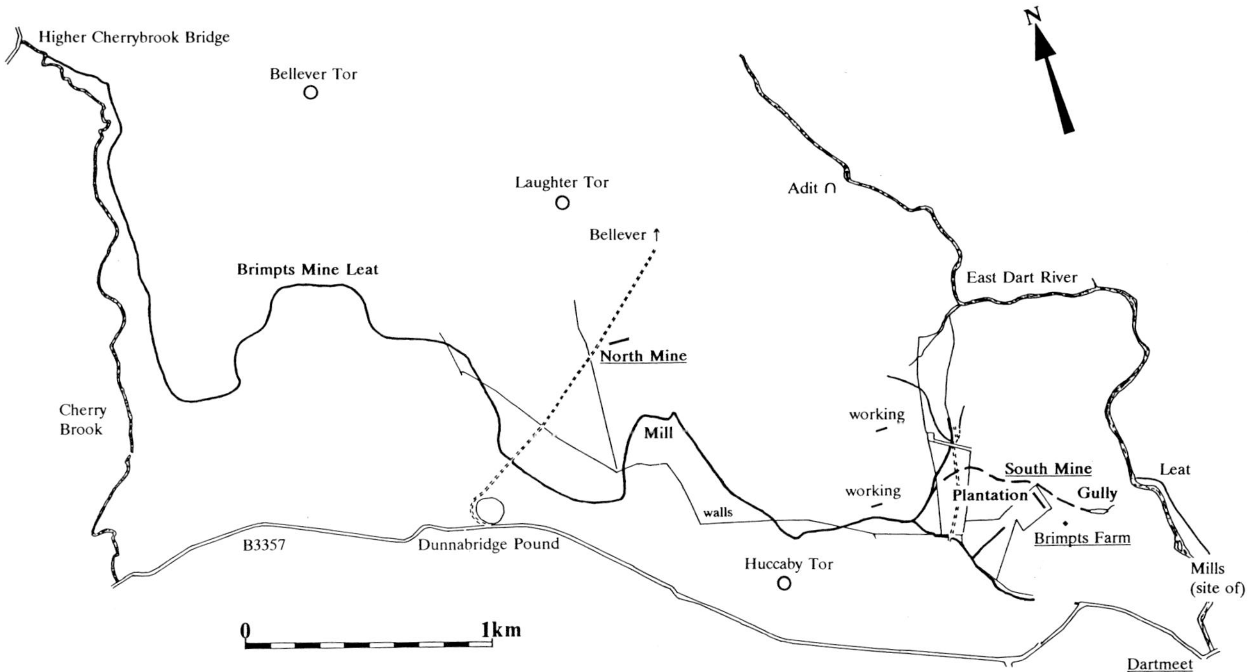

Fig. 1. Map of the Brimpts Tin Mining Sett.
(Brimpts Farm is at NGR SX 668738)

The History of the Brimpts Tin Mines

Notes: The units used at the time for measurement and currency have been retained for this narrative. These were fathoms (fm), feet (ft) and inches (in), where 1 fathom = 6 feet = 72 inches = 1.83 metres; and pounds (*£ or l*), shillings (*s*) and pence (*d*) where £1 or 1*l* = 20*s* = 240*d*. The terminology of the miners has also largely been maintained - see the Glossary for terms not explained in the text.

As is commonly the case, the early history of Brimpts is sparsely documented. The earliest references linking tin with Brimpts are from the coinage rolls, the records of tin metal submitted for payment of tax thereon. These mention Robert Hexta of Bremelstonte in 1456[1], Robert Hexta of Bremst in 1470[2] and later, John Hexte of Bremston in 1523[3]. There is no evidence that this tin came from Brimpts itself, but the references usefully demonstrate the variability of early versions of the name.

In a lease dated the 1st January 1514[4], in the reign of Henry VIII, an acre of land at "Dertameta" (Dartmeet) was rented to Christopher Prous and Richard Hamelyn who had recently built there a "blowyng myll & knakkyng myll", i.e. a furnace for smelting and a stamping mill for crushing the ore prior to concentrating the tin. Sufficient information is given in the lease for the site to be identified with certainty as that now occupied by Badger's Holt Café at Dartmeet. A blowing mill alone could have been supplied from tin-streaming operations, but the contemporaneous stamping mill points to the processing of lode (vein) material which had to be crushed to liberate the cassiterite, the tin oxide, from the rock. Tin content is generally quite low, the volume of rock to be handled large, so the mills would have been sited as close as practicable to the main ore source and no site is more conveniently close to the Dartmeet mills than the workings at Brimpts, making a link probable.

At that time, the ore would have been dug from an openwork, a shallow surface working along the line of the lode. Such workings were given a name with the ending -beme and in a will dated 1531[5], Sir John Shilston left to his wife a number of tin workings in Devonshire including a "Brymstebeme". We believe this was the name given to the long narrow openwork between Brimpts Farm and the East Dart River and that the ore was taken across the river at Smethford, a ford mentioned in the lease and just above the mills.

In the early 17th century, a list[6] of the many tin workings in which a Richard Stuckey held a share includes, under Ashburton Stannary Court, an "Ester (East) Brymstorbeme adioyninge to Wyndyatts Crosse". We associate Brymstorbeme with Brimpts on the basis of early spelling variants, but there is always the possibility of error, confusion for example with Brimstone Down near Chagford, so any supporting information is useful. Unfortunately, the location of Wyndyatts Crosse is not known to the authors. Our belief is that Ester Brymstorbeme is another name for the lower openwork and that the Ester implies another adjacent openwork such as Wester Brymstorbeme which is likely to have been the site above Brimpts Farm later called the plantation. This would place Wyndyatts Crosse at Brimpts Farm itself, which is quite feasible as the difficulty of crossing the main River Dart made the Dartmeet area a crossing place of many routes in addition to the local tracks to Babeny corn mill and the ancient tenements. The name Windeatt (modern form) was common in the area, Widecombe registers recording the name as far back as 1560.

On the basis of this scant information, it appears that the workings at Brimpts itself had started by about 1513 and were operated through to perhaps the early 17th century.

The Widecombe registers have a much later entry dated 16th January 1708 mentioning Leonard Kent, a tinner, at Brimpt[7]. Like the Hexte references, this refers to Brimpts as a residence and he could have been working elsewhere. There is no other evidence to support tin mining there at that time.

At the end of 1797, Rev. John Swete on his tour of Devon[8] wrote that "At Brimpse, ... Mr Sanders of Exeter, the Owner and a Gentleman of considerable information .... informed me he had collected pieces of ore, which he considered to be rich in Metal, and which might instigate him to commence "adventurer", as he conceived from the Specimens He had found, and their locality, a lode must necessarily be at a short distance." Mr Sanders did indeed start mining operations as evidenced by the declaration of Richard Tuckett in April 1849[9];-

"I, Richard Tuckett of Dunnabridge in the parish of Lidford,

yeoman, do solemnly declare that I am now 79 years of age and that about 50 years since I was in the service of Mr Joseph Sanders of Brimpts and that whilst in his employ I was in the habit of drawing with a slide-but tin stuff from the shaft near to the stable, and also from a level in a field called the Potatoe Field, part of Brimpts estate, down to the stumps, and I continued drawing tin stuff from these places for two or three years. And I further declare that I remember the mine at Brimpts being worked by Joseph Sanders alone for 7 or 8 years and that the tin stuff when made marketable was taken to Tavistock, and I further declare that Joseph Sanders discontinued working the mine because he considered that the miners were imposing on him, and I recollect that the miners offered to work the mine at a low tribute but that Joseph Sanders refused their application. 4th April 1849."*
(*Not literally alone, we assume, as Joseph Sanders was a banker in Exeter as well as running the Brimpts Estate.)

The shaft near the stable, later called the engine shaft, was at the top of the gully (see Fig. 8.). A wheelpit in the north side of the gully is aligned with this shaft and is believed to have powered pumps to drain the workings which reputedly went down to 10fms below adit level which was itself 16fms below the surface. The Potatoe (*sic*) Field level is identifiable as the shallow adit under the plantation (see Fig. 9.), so mining took place under both early openwork sites and a location marked as "old shaft" on a later plan suggests exploration (at least) on the south side of the valley below Brimpts too.

According to the Tuckett declaration, the mine had 'stumps' (*sic*) i.e. a stamping mill, and must have had an associated dressing floor. Logically these would have been either between the two main workings or at the bottom of the gully as both sites have the right combination of flat area and sloping ground to site a waterwheel, but the actual location has not so far been identified with certainty.

The two waterwheels required a water supply greater than the small stream at Brimpts Farm could supply so a leat was cut starting from the Cherry Brook just below the higher bridge (near Powdermills) and following a winding 4 mile (6.5km) route over common land and through newtakes to the mine. The leat was mentioned in connection with a dispute concerning Owlacombe Mine in 1836[10] and was said to have been cut by Nicholas Fezzy "30 years ago".

When Joseph Sanders started the mine, he was no doubt influenced by work in progress at Bachelor's Hall and particularly by the successes at Vitifer, but Richard Tuckett's declaration indicates a lack of profitability and this is supported by a comment in the Duchy's Dartmoor Proceedings where "Brent's Mine" was said to be "not very prosperous"[11] in 1799. The agent then was named as Samuel Date. Taken with John Swete's reference, this suggests mining started in 1798. A table in Lysons' 1822 volume on Devonshire gives the date when Brempts last worked as 1807.

After Joseph Sander's opposition, no further work was done until in 1848, William Rowland, a miller, and Martin Dunn, mine agent, both of Holne were granted a one year licence of the mine by the Duchy from 1st November[12].

In *Mining Journal* of 8th September 1849, Brimpts Tin Mining Company published its manifesto. This was designed to attract investors by painting a glowing picture regardless of hard fact. For instance, you will read that the East and West Dart Rivers "furnish sufficient waterpower for all the requisite purposes", whereas in reality these were at the lowest part of the mining sett and were never able to be utilised, so read on with caution!

"Brimpts Tin Mining Company, Dartmoor, Devon.
At work on the Cost-Book principle which exempts shareholders from any liability beyond the amount of their shares and enables them to withdraw at any time by giving notice to the purser to that effect.
In 256 shares at 2l. 2s each.
No shareholder to hold less than 4/256ths.
Bankers. Devon and Cornwall Banking Company, Exeter and Totnes.
Solicitor. Mr R. Robins, Tavistock.
Purser. Mr George Stranger, Holne, Nr Ashburton.
Secretary pro tem. Mr R. Tripp, Exeter.
Offices. Bedford Chambers, Bamphylde St..

This mine is situated at the bottom of Dartmeet Hill in the Forest of Dartmoor in the parish of Lidford, Devon, distant 16m from Exeter, 12 from Tavistock, 12 from Totnes.

The sett is about a mile long from east to west and half a mile wide. There are several lodes passing through it in an east and west direction which have been worked on by the late owner of the estate whence considerable returns were made; and no doubt exists that this mine will again take its stand as one of the most productive and richest mines in the county.

The subjoined report of Mr John Hitchins (one of the most eminent practical miners of the day) and also the declaration of Mr Tuckett, made before a Master Extraordinary in Chancery - that the mine was worked about 50y since and that it was abandoned by him solely for the reason therein stated - furnishes indisputable evidence of its great value.

As the meeting of the shareholders is to take place at the mine on the 27th Sept., for the purposes of carrying on the operations of the mine, applications for shares must be made before the 22nd Sept., to Mr R. Tripp, Exeter.

(The declaration of Richard Tuckett was included here - see p7.)

The Old Brimpts Mine Sett. *Report.*

Sir. Having carefully examined this sett, and noted its various points, as far as they admitted of inspection, with a view to submit my opinion thereon as to the probability of its future productiveness and capabilities, permit me to offer the following observations:-

In the first place, - independent of living evidence - the ancient workings show that a vast amount of labour must have been bestowed on searching for ore, and from the sides of the excavations, stones of tin of rich quality have been found - clearly showing that was the metal sought for, and that a great quantity must have been raised; in fact, the renown of this mine has been the theme sounding in my ears since my first recollection of my late father having, both from report as well as personal inspection, often expressed to me his desire to obtain the grant; nor do I myself the least dispute the correctness of his opinion, for I believe the lode, or rather lodes, are large and must have been productive.

The Sett is an extensive and sufficient one for the employment of capital, I think beneficially, as well as the exercise of mining skill, being from North to South from Bellevor Torr to Dartmeet, and from the East to West Dart Rivers, which furnish sufficient waterpower for all requisite purposes - such as pumping the water and drawing the stuff and work out of the mine, as well as every purpose of dressing.

There is also timber of every description growing close on the mine, and the stratum of ground through which the lodes traverse is of a soft and congenial character, so that this adventure can be carried out with all due economy. I am informed that the mine is 10fm under the adit. I should therefore advise a water-wheel to be at once provided, with all the requisite appliances, either new or good second-hand as the case turns out, and to clear and drive the adit level. Also clear up the shafts and workings, so as to be satisfied as to the whereabouts to begin operations for a permanent working, which if properly carried out, I am of opinion will lead to satisfactory results.

In conclusion, allow me to say, this sett, from the foregoing imperfect sketch of its prospects, is such as I should not hesitate to recommend to any spirited set of adventurers to whom I should wish success and I remain.
Sir, your obedient servant, JOHN HITCHINS, Tavistock July 1849."*
(*John appears to be an error for Jehu.)

By the 29th September, all the shares had been sold and Mr Hitchins had been engaged to supervise the workings[13].

The first objective was to clear the old workings in the gully and on the 15th March 1850, Captain John Key reported that the deep adit level had been reopened for a distance of 45fm, leaving just 3fm to reach the engine shaft[14]. At the same time, the first 12fm of the engine shaft itself had been cleared, leaving just 4fm down to adit level. So almost all of the above-adit area of the gully had become available again, but not the deep workings.

In the plantation (the "potatoe field"), they had "opened on the lode and have broken excellent stones of tin".

Progress seems to have been promising, so it is perhaps surprising that it was only after nearly eleven months work, in August 1850, that they decided to cut a leat and erect machinery to process the large quantity of tin stuff broken underground[15]. It was claimed that the value of the tin stuff raised was equal to the capital expenditure of less than £150. The shareholders were even told that a dividend could be expected once the stamps were erected.

In November 1850, further progress was reported with ore raised valued at £250 against an expenditure of £300 which included the cost of cutting the leat and purchasing the machinery[16]. This equipment would have been the waterwheel, wheelpit, stamps and dressing floor on a new site in the plantation. Clearly this required a new branch from the 1798 leat route, but was a whole new leat cut as the report implies? The first half of the original was probably just put back into good order, but in the central section, a new route has been cut about 5m from the old leat, on the downslope side. As this new cut approaches Huccaby Tor, it diverges from the old route, enhancing the gradient slightly. Shortly after, the old route falls to a junction with the new.

An unfortunate break now occurs in reports about "Old Brimpts" as it was called, usually a sign of problems, but the 4th September 1851 report is still optimistic[17]. An abundant supply of ore is noted, so much in fact that the stamps have a three months backlog. A new sett is also being developed in the newtake near Laughter Tor and a call (demand for extra capital) of 10 shillings per share is issued to purchase a new wheel and twelve stamps' head for this. In the meantime, payment of a dividend remains elusive. But was the situation as rosy as the report for the shareholders' benefit implied?

Certainly something seems to have been amiss, because over the next few months, no less than three independent expert opinions were sought on the mines' prospects[18] (these were not printed in *Mining Journal* until July 1852). The reports are extremely useful in giving us a comprehensive assessment of the mines in the winter of 1851/2.

At the gully, there were two main lodes plus a lesser one, all running W-E. The deep adit entrance at the river end gave access onto the north lode which it followed for a distance before taking a cross passage to follow the south lode, passing the engine shaft and continuing into the hillside below Brimpts Farm for a total distance of about 120fm. This site reportedly produced good specimens of tin ore, but there is no indication that any attempt was made to drain the old sub-adit workings so there must be doubt about whether the prospects were as bright as painted, the bulk of ore having presumably been removed by earlier miners. Nevertheless, there were suggested advances in two directions, firstly downwards towards a projected lode junction at 35 to 40fm depth and secondly, a continuation of the deep adit until under the plantation workings where it would not only expose those lodes at depth, but also drain all the plantation levels of present and future operations.

The plantation workings were at this time the most productive part of the mines. An adit level about 100fm long had been driven along the course of a roughly N-S caunter lode (i.e. a lode running across the main W-E trend) and in so doing, had intersected three W-E lodes, the junction with the south lode producing "very good work" (this south lode was presumed to be a continuation of the gully south lode, hence the same name). A large quantity of tin stuff from here was at surface, large heaps were in the level and two pitches had been set out for stoping (mining of the lode itself). Nowhere however is any estimate given for the tin content of this ore so the value is undefinable. In the centre of the workings, a shaft was being sunk to explore below adit level and during the winter, a chain of flat-rods was set up from the plantation waterwheel to power pumps in this shaft. It was 7fm below adit level in March 1852.

The third working, in the newtake, was on a site that shows considerable evidence (in the form of a line of excavations with many trial pits extending beyond the two ends) of having been worked at shallow depth (less than 10m) probably in the 16th/17th centuries. The 19th century working commenced in the centre of this line with the sinking of a shaft and driving of a cross-cut adit from a point lower down the hillside. Early results from here indicated an estimated 5 to 7 cwts of black tin to every 100 sacks of 12 gallons each (about 5% black tin), which was a promising figure. By March 1852, the shaft was down 14fm and power for the pumps was supplied via nearly 200fm of flat-rods powered by a 24ft by 3½ft waterwheel fed with water from the Brimpts mine leat which fortuitously passed below the new mine.

A second site is mentioned in connection with the newtake in the report by Adam Murray. It is not described there, but Duchy records of May 1852 name it as the East Dart River lode[19]. This, we suppose, refers to the exploratory adit in Winford Newtake, but since no other information is given, it is uncertain whether this was a new venture or an extension of an existing adit.

So we can summarise the situation by saying that the old gully workings were probably exhausted of tin but development of new workings was contemplated, the plantation was producing much ore, but of unspecified grade, and was being developed and the North Mine site (to use the later name) looked promising, but required capital investment to develop it. The three reports on the mining prospects, by James Carpenter, John Kneebone and Adam Murray were therefore favourable, but were opinions sought by the management and hence open to bias.

In March 1852, matters started to come to a head with a meeting described as long and stormy "and a few anathemas were poured up on the head of Mr Irish, one of the projectors"[20].

Two months later, at the next meeting[21], "it was resolved that, in the present state of the Company's finances, a large number of shareholders not having paid their calls, it is deemed advisable to discontinue the working of the mine. The plant, machinery and materials will be sold by auction ....". A committee was formed to wind up the affairs of the mine and the captain resigned[22].

The advertisement for sale of Old Brimpts Mine in June[23], lists the following:-
2 waterwheels of 28ft and 25ft diameter and 4ft breast.
270fms of rods, pulleys and stands.
2 bobs and rods in shafts, 2 lifts of pumps.
6 head of stamps, attached to wheel.
Dressing department complete.
Whim and rope pulleys, capstan and rope.
Smith's tools and the usual materials of a mine in full work.

Of these materials, we can identify the 28ft wheel, the stamps, 70fm of rods etc., 1 bob and pump plus the dressing department as belonging to the plantation, the 25ft wheel, 200fm of rods etc., 1 bob and 1 pump as at North Mine, with nothing relatable to the gully at all.

It seems likely that the Old Brimpts management anticipated the closure and sought new backers for on July 7th, James Carpenter wrote a report on the "Duke of Cornwall" tin mine[24] and in *Mining Journal* for the 17th July, a manifesto was published for the Duke of Cornwall Consolidated Tin Mining Company. This describes the sett and its bounds before making two interesting statements, the first of which describes Brimpts tin as "being of the richest character, and producing on an average 50*l* per ton". This is the only reference we have to the price or quantity of tin sold by the previous company. It claimed sales, but appeared reluctant to publicise these. The second statement was later to be proven disastrously wrong;- "A matter of the greatest importance to the economical working of the mine is the possession of unlimited water power, equal to the utmost requirements of the mine ...".

The manifesto, incorporating the three reports mentioned earlier (Carpenter, Kneebone and Murray) plus the verbose statement of Jehu Hitchins from 1849, was offering 1000 shares of £1 each. It seems unlikely that this was raised since nothing further was reported by this Company and there are indications in later documents that the sett fell into disuse.

By the next January however, a third company, the Devon Tin Mines, was offering in its manifesto up to 10000 shares of £1 with a minimum of £3000 capital on start-up, of which over £2000 had already been raised[25]. For the first time, this was a London-based company with shareholders mainly in London and the Southeast. It used as its bankers Messrs Strahan, Paul & Co., a partner in which, Mr R. M. Bates, was also a Devon Tin shareholder. A member of the local committee was William Wills Esq., who had previously served on the committees of both former companies.

On the 10th March 1853[26], Devon Tin had enough capital to proceed and held its first general meeting, electing Mr J. Ware as mine captain. The shareholders decided an estimate for the work for the mines should be obtained, considered and agreed upon. The plan for the mines was to sink North Mine deeper and develop further levels, whilst at the gully, the flooded engine shaft was to be drained to gain access to the sub-adit levels.

In mid-May[27], when a deputation of shareholders visited the mines accompanied by Mr Jehu Hitchins, work was in progress at North Mine with good tin stuff being raised from the east end of the 5fm level whilst below, the 15fm level was being driven through hard ground. At the gully, the bob pit was being excavated prior to collaring the shaft. Forges had been provided at both mines. Captain Williams of the Arundell Mines (a copper mine near Ashburton, later Druid Mine) visited the sett also and expressed his satisfaction at the progress made.

It was at the next meeting however, on the 28th May[28], that some interesting information emerged. Firstly, it was revealed that "this enterprise has been undertaken by the spirited company of capitalists who are engaged in developing the Arundell Copper Mines", so both setts were effectively under the same management, hence the request to Captain Williams to periodically visit Brimpts. Mr Amery, the Arundell freeholder was introduced and spoke of setting up a benevolent fund and a library for the miners.

The report of the deputation that had visited the mines was read, recommending amongst other things, the erection of miners' cottages. Mr Adam Murray (the producer of an earlier mine report, now a shareholder and committee member) suggested an estimate be obtained for 10 cottages at about £25 each (times have changed!).

No mention of the plantation was made in earlier proposals and Mr Murray was now advising caution in respect of sinking the shaft further. We don't know why this site so suddenly went out of favour, but it is likely that Brimpts Tin had exploited all the worthwhile reserves.

Some 200 sacks of tin stuff had been raised from the 5fm level at North Mine having an average of 3½cwt of tin per 100 sacks. This was ready for stamping (but there were no stamps there at that time). Some ore had been dressed and a small portion on show was given an estimated value of £40 per ton.

On the same day, James Ware, the captain, reported having "blasted a hole in the lode in the 15fm level and it produced good saving stuff". This is the only record of the use of explosives at the mines. The rate of driving the levels quoted in later reports suggests that much of the work was by manual methods only. This seems strangely inefficient, but Devon Tin was using the Cornish 'tutwork' system where work at the mine was divided up and offered as a set of short-term contracts at an open auction. Small teams of miners would bid competitively for each contract and the captain would then offer the work to the lowest bidder, sometimes at a lower rate than that bid. The successful team was then paid per linear fathom cut for drives or shafts and per fathom cube for stoping the lode. Out of this was deducted the cost of materials used such as candles and powder, the cost of drawing and landing the ore, the smiths' fees and other sundries. This system kept wage costs to the minimum and the miners on the poverty line, so powder would only have been used where it was most cost-effective.

With Capt. Williams' agreement, driving of the 5fm level was suspended to permit North Mine shaft to be cased and divided "that the stuff may be drawn with horses" i.e. by erection of a horse whim. Six men were employed to drive the 15fm level at £18 per fm cut.

Towards the end of June[29], work was approaching completion at South Mine (as the old workings at Brimpts itself were now called) to couple the wheel in the plantation to the balance bob and pump in the gully engine shaft by a long line of flat-rods. The line went first to the site of the plantation shaft which was by now abandoned and was there turned through a 55° angle by a v-bob, before descending the hillside to the gully, initially in a slight cutting, then on stands well above ground level.

At North Mine, work was still in progress in both the 5 and 15fm levels and the casing, dividing and installation of a footway was also approaching completion. The difference in the nature of the rock in the 5 and 15fm levels was illustrated by the letting of the 5 at £4 4*s* per fm as compared to the earlier £18 per fm for the 15.

In early July[30], at South Mine, the lift of pumps was lowered into the engine shaft and on the 14th[31], the (plantation) wheel was started "to fork the water" and pump the old workings dry for, it appears, the first time since abandonment in 1807. The assembly worked remarkably well and enabled progress to start on casing, dividing, installing footways and erecting a whim. This was a critical moment, because the whole future of South Mine depended on what was found. It is most frustrating therefore that the next report we have is not until 26th September 1853[32] when it is stated briefly that repairs to the stamps at South Mine had just been completed. That meant that at South Mine all the surface facilities were in place, but was the investment there going to be profitable?

On the 7th November 1853[33], a general meeting of the shareholders was held which revealed that of the original £4065 capital, £1454 18*s* 7*d* had been expended so far. One of the shareholders, Mr Brown, sparked a considerable discussion by complaining that so large an expenditure had occurred without the express sanction of the shareholders especially since this was the first supposedly bi-monthly meeting since May. The committee presented its excuses and concurred that the meetings should in future be held regularly. The low price of shares formed another subject for comment.

There was then a comprehensive presentation on the state of the mines, including plans and sections prepared by Mr Gulley of Tavistock. South Mine facilities were described and the engine shaft was stated as down to 25fm 3ft 11in, "the lode presented a kindly appearance, producing stones of tin of a rich quality". Now this was much the same depth reported from the *c*1800 operations, so no great advance had been made and nothing was included in *Mining Journal* about the findings in any old workings below adit level.

At North Mine, progress was being made. On the surface, a new smiths' shop had been erected and enlargements made to the carpenters' workplace and materials store. Stamps and dressing floors were being provided, but were incomplete. Underground, the 5 and 15 fm levels had been extended, the 15fm east being then 11fm long, driven through hard ground, the lode producing good stones of tin, the 15fm west was in 9fm 3ft, the ground of a favourable character for mineral and producing some tin. In the 5fm level, a winze was being sunk to the 15fm level. This was east of the engine shaft and the flat-rods had been extended from there to pump this new underground shaft dry.

Then came a small but significant admission, progress had been retarded by having insufficient water to drive both wheels. Adverse weather was blamed for hampering remedial work, but was this the real reason?

The shareholders were not entirely happy with the situation and decided to seek an independent report on the state and prospects of the mines, ruling that in the meantime, expenditure be minimised. Mr Samuel Perkes C.E., a shareholder, was asked to visit the mines in his professional capacity as an engineer and prepare the report, the meeting being adjourned until the 22nd November.

At the resumed meeting[34], Mr Perkes presented a most comprehensive report which is reproduced here in full because of its importance:-

"In compliance with your instructions I visited the above mines (Devon Tin) on the 15th instant, with a view to examine into the general nature of the workings of the mines, and more particularly into the nature of the machinery at present employed, and its capability for converting the produce of your mines into a marketable state, and beg to lay before you the result of my investigations thereon. The sett is divided into two separate and distinct operations, and designated the North Mine and the South Mine, each of which I shall report upon separately. The North Mine comprises one engine-shaft, which is now 15fm. deep, and from which is driven, at 5fm. in depth, one adit 44fm. due east and 20fm. west, also a 15fm. level driven east about 11fm., and 10fm. west; the whole on the course of the lode, which varies from 15 to 24in. thick. In the bottom of the 5 east there is a communication with the winze-shaft, which is now sunk 4fm. below the 5fm. level, making a total of 9fm. in depth; this shaft ought, in my opinion, to be the main engine-shaft, and to form the centre of your future operations, as from all appearance it will doubtless intersect the slide (apparently a fault cutting the surface a little east of the engine shaft and dipping eastwards at about 45°) *at 25fm. deep, and which runs north and south, consequently it intersects the east and west lodes at about right angles, and when this slide is intersected by the winze-shaft, as expected at the 25fm., there is no doubt but very rich ore will be met with, as the appearances of the numerous lodes are extremely favourable, and what is already raised contains a considerable quantity of very fine tin, the poorest of which will yield about 1cwt. of tin to every 100 sacks of ore, and each sack will weigh upon the average about 1¼cwt., but the average quality now being raised from the winze will yield about 2 to 2½cwt. of tin to the 100 sacks, thus it will be seen that the quality is very rapidly improving, and from which I had stamped and washed when at the mines the sample which I now produce, and there is now at the surface about 500 sacks all ready for stamping, but which cannot be accomplished unless either the operations at South Mine are suspended, or else*

more power provided, the latter of which I most strongly recommend. The power at the North Mine consists of one water-wheel, 20-ft. diameter, and about 3-ft. breast, which is fed by a leet cut along the slope of the hill about 190fm. below the present engine and winze-shafts, and down each of which is placed a pump with 6-inch working barrels, and which are worked by means of chain-rods, communicating with and attached to the water-wheel, which is of sufficient power only to work the two pumps as at present existing, whose small dimensions cannot be supposed to be sufficient for the increased depth of shaft which will ultimately be required for the practical development of the vast mineral wealth which is plainly foreshadowed in every part of the excavations, and which evidently improve as they extend. Adjoining this water-wheel preparations are made for erecting six stamps' heads, and the turn-barrel for which is already erected; and at some 50ft. below the water-wheel there is now prepared, and nearly completed, the dressing-floor. The whole of these arrangements are so far satisfactory, and will do exceedingly well for the purposes intended, provided there was sufficient power to work the stamps, which cannot be done unless the mining operations and pumping are suspended, which it would be very injudicious to do. Therefore, it will be necessary forthwith to prepare another wheel of sufficient power to work the pumps, the winding-gear for the shafts, and the stamps for dressing the ores - say, a wheel not less than 50-feet diameter, and 6-feet breast, and plant the same on the same spot as the 20-feet wheel, which can be easily accomplished by lowering the wheel-pit 15ft., and the whole of the present pumping gear, stamps, and winding gear, can be attached and worked at the same time, without any stoppage or hindrance to any portion thereof (from site knowledge, the authors believe this would have been far more difficult and disruptive than Mr Perkes indicates).

Whilst the change of wheels is being effected, the present winze-shaft can be stripped down at the upper part thereof to 9ft. by 6 ft., and divided off by a common brattice 3 feet for the footway and pumps, and properly stay the same for the permanent main shaft, which can easily be effected; whilst at so shallow a depth as the bottom portion thereof is amply large enough for that purpose already, and down which will ultimately be required a 12-in. pump, instead of the 6-inch, as at present. By this arrangement the standing expense of a horse and driver at the hoisting-whim can be dispensed with, and the whole of the ores worked daily as they are raised from the mine. A small tramway will also be necessary to run the ores from the shaft to the stamps, which will be of very trifling expense, but which will save much labour and cartage. The 15fm. level is at present within 15 fathoms from the winze-shaft, and the quantity of ore already in sight can be excavated and brought to surface at any time required, and which is of a quality that will well pay for working, although so near the surface.

The carpenters' shop and sawpit, just now completed, together with the smiths' shop, office, and store, are very serviceable buildings of their kinds, and will well answer their intended purpose; but some provision will be necessary to protect the banksmen from the inclemency of the weather, which is inconceivably severe in that district: some plain rough boarding will be sufficient, as a kind of rough shed, over the shaft, or else a common thatched roof. It will also be necessary for a couple of labourers to be employed for about two months or so in widening the upper end of the leet, in order to collect a little more water for the wheel, which, together with the wheel at the plantation, and which also is fed from the same leet, is not over and above well supplied, as either one or the other is frequently obliged to go short, hence they are not doing full duty.

The South Mine consists of one well-constructed engine-shaft, 25fm. deep, and in which is placed some good pumping gear: from this shaft an adit level is driven west, at 16fm. deep, for 22fm., and below which there is an ancient adit level at about 16fm. west, and through which the water is directed as pumped from the mine. The pumps are worked by a connection of rods carried up to the water-wheel in the plantation, and attached to which are six stamps and a dressing-floor, but which stamps cannot be worked unless the whole of the operations in the South Mine are stopped, as there is not power to work the stamps and pumps, in consequence of the heavy but unavoidable drag of the long line of connecting-rods leading from the pump at the shaft to the water-wheel in the plantation. Therefore, as there are some ores now raised at this mine containing small portions of tin, and as there is every prospect of an increase as the works extend, I recommend that the small wheel which I propose to remove from the North Mine be fixed in the ancient gully, where a wheel has been worked before, as every preparation for the approach and discharge of the water-wheel, pit, &c., is still in existence, and ready for immediate use. Therefore, I would recommend you to still maintain the plantation wheel, and use it exclusively for pumping the south shaft as at present employed, and which is all that it is capable of doing. Then, by fixing this small wheel in the ancient gully, as proposed (and which adjoins the south shaft), and attaching thereto the stamp-heads from the plantation wheel (where they are now fixed, but cannot be worked), you will have the means at once of stamping the produce of this mine also without loss of time, cartage, or hindrance, as fast as the ores are raised, and the whole of which transformation will not exceed about 600l. in cost, but without which you cannot efficiently work your mines, much less dress the ores, the value of which will assist in defraying the expense of developing the mine. (Coupling the wheel in the gully to the pumps and thus leaving the plantation wheel to drive its attached stamps seems more feasible and eliminates the flat-rods.) *The present laborious and expensive mode of dressing the ores will require your serious attention, as there is a great expense of labour and loss of time in obtaining the results. If the produce of ores increase, of which there is every moral certainty, it will be necessary to adopt a more simple and efficient means of effecting this object than at present in use, and of which I shall be happy to advise you when necessary.*

The next point I most earnestly recommend to your consideration is the necessity of providing some description of cottages as residences for the men employed in these mines, and whose destitute condition renders them objects of your serious attention, as there are no dwellings within many miles of their work wherein these poor men can lay their heads. I have examined the small piece of land near to the Dart, which I am informed you have secured with a view to carrying out that object, and I consider it very well adapted for the erection of some cottages, which can be constructed for about 80l. each, and one for the captain for about 120l. and for which a rental equal to five per cent. on the cost would be given, and would thus induce steady men and their families to come and reside near their work, but without such accommodation, steady constant labour cannot be obtained, as none but careless, indifferent tramps will take up with the employment in such a district, and who seldom remain more than a week or two at most. Your captain (Ware) I consider a very steady industrious man, but whose family is now obliged to reside some 16 miles distant, in consequence of not being able to get accommodation nearer, and which renders it exceeding uncomfortable, and frequently very difficult for him to attend to his duties as he is desirous of doing. I further beg to suggest for your consideration the necessity of some practical and competent person to visit the mines once every month, to advise with your captain as to the best course to be pursued with the works, the best means of obtaining materials, the best markets to obtain such materials from, adjusting the prices of that work, &c., for the men, to examine the nature of the work, and to check over the amount done, and to advise as to the best mode of continuing or abandoning any portion of the operations, and to take a strict account of all matters relating thereto upon the spot, and furnish a proper report thereof to, and personally attend, every monthly meeting, so to be enabled at once to answer any question in relation to the mines which may be required, and thus to form a kind of responsible connecting link between the shareholders and the works, and to see that their wishes are faithfully carried out; and by such means I doubt not but great good will result, and much expense be saved to the proprietors, and that satisfaction ensured which cannot be obtained by any other means, and which would by far outweigh the trifling expense which would thus be incurred.

In having examined over every part of the workings, both underground and over, and having traversed through every adit and level, I can only say that I, as a shareholder, am more than satisfied of the legitimacy and bona fide nature of this adventure, and consider that we have to prepare ourselves, from all appearances, for a very lucrative undertaking; but I beg the shareholders not to be too anxious for returns, which would only defeat the ends in view, as it is well known to all persons acquainted with mining that with so small an outlay which has been expended in commencing the opening of these mines, nothing extraordinary must be expected at present; but with the judicious expenditure of capital in extending their development, and providing for dressing the ores when obtained, the most ample returns will ultimately be given; but considering the small outlay which has been made, I consider that under the circumstances you have ample value given, but a considerable further outlay must be made and patience exercised before you are able to reap the fruits of your labours, which are now fast ripening into maturity; and I cannot but congratulate the shareholders upon the valuable property which this adventure can scarcely fail at no very distant day to prove itself, and which I am strongly of opinion will yield the most ample returns for all the money and labour expended upon it.

I cannot conclude this report without alluding to a circumstance which strongly impressed itself on my mind when at the mines, and one which deeply concerns all interested in this undertaking - viz., in looking over the refuse material as taken from the excavations, I was forcibly struck with its appearance, particularly the decomposed granite, of which there is a very large quantity, not only on the surface, but in the mines also, and from the sides of the excavations, in which I found it so soft as to be able to scrape it away with my hand, and thus removed several handfulls, and upon close examination with a powerful microscope, I am fully disposed to believe it to be auriferous; therefore I selected a quantity, and placed it in the charge of Capt. Ware, and shall be glad if you will consent that about one ton weight be delivered to me, together with some quicksilver, at your earliest convenience, and upon receipt of which I will undertake to pulverise and amalgamate it in one of my patented amalgamating machines, which will instantly test it, upon a practical working scale, whether it does or does not contain gold, and if so, the precise quantity per ton. I do not wish to raise expectations, for fear of disappointment; but from numerous other trials I have practically made, I am inclined to think that this material is really worth the trial which I will make, free of expense, upon receipt of the above."

So, despite all the earlier pronouncements of unlimited water power, it was now clear that the mine machinery was drastically under-supplied and under-powered, with enough water at times to drive only one wheel. Even worse, each wheel was insufficiently powerful to drive both stamps and pumps. Mr Perkes had a solution that would cause serious disruption and require capital investment if implemented, but without it, the mines would be crippled. And then there was the new twist to the story, the possibility of gold. A period of reflection was called for.

Technically, development work had now been suspended, but work continued underground and on the dressing floors[35], seemingly raising and dressing the accessible ore.

Despite the problems, morale seems still to have been high and, according to a quotation by A. K. Hamilton Jenkin in his description of the Arundell Mine[36], "A similar feast took place that night (Christmas Eve, 1853) at the Devon Tin Mines on Dartmoor which was under the auspices of the same company. Here the menu consisted of a large side of Wiltshire bacon together with a 60lb American cheese, while each man was offered the choice of a Guernsey frock (jersey) or a woollen waistcoat. Both mines were in advance of their time in possessing a benevolent fund and as there had been no serious accident at either during the year a portion of this was distributed 'in a genial way' at these Christmas gatherings, leaving a balance in hand of £100 at the Arundell Mine and about £20 in the fund of the Devon Tin Mines."

The euphoria soon collapsed though when, at the end of December, frost and severe snowstorms froze the water in the leat and filled it with snow[37]. The miners soon became concerned about the lack of work and some were temporarily employed driving the South Mine deep adit. It was suggested that the East Dart River lode be explored further by a couple of men[38].

The first meeting of 1854 was on the 19th January[39]. There was a further review of the current state of the mines and plans for future working, but strangely, nothing was reported about Mr Perkes' solution to the crisis. Instead the meeting seems to have been totally distracted by the gold discovery question. Mr Perkes revealed that from 7lb of decomposed granite he had extracted 5½grs of gold which he showed the meeting. At a rate of more than 3oz to the ton (0.011%), Mr Perkes thought that a large scale trial was justified. In order to confirm this valuable discovery, the committee had submitted two other samples for independent assay. One produced a zero result, the other 4dwts 9grs per ton (This latter assay is a troy weight equivalent to 6.8 parts per million. Mr Perkes' 5½grs in 7lb was probably avoirdupois, giving 112ppm, a huge difference, but from a carefully selected sample.). This led to a lengthened discussion and an agreement to send 30 to 40 tons of decomposed granite for processing. With apparent prospects of producing both tin and gold, the shareholders appeared highly satisfied. Subsequently however, there was no further mention of gold so whilst it was undoubtedly present, we must presume that the bulk trial was unsuccessful.

Following this meeting, reports from Devon Tin for 1854 are minimal. Mine captain James Ware vanished and was replaced by William Thomas of the Arundell Copper Mine[40].

South Mine development remained suspended whilst at North Mine, sinking of the winze was resumed[41]. During the year, it passed the 15 fm level and was continued down to an intended new level at 27fm. As it went, prospects appeared to increase. The lode was first said to produce good tinwork, "opening ground that will pay well for working at a good profit", then, by September 13th, the leader of tin was described as very rich.

On September 28th, a committee meeting was held[42], but the report makes no mention of the mines themselves! It did reveal though that financially a crisis was approaching. From an initial balance of £1645 7*s* 6*d*, labour had cost £212 8*s* 2*d* in March, £188 0*s* 2*d* in April, £141 2*s* 10*d* in May, £73 0*s* 5*d* in June, £94 4*s* 8*d* in July, £78 1*s* 11*d* in August and £98 9*s* 10*d* in September. With other costs, this left a balance of £657 13*s* 6*d*, enough to last only a few more months. What the shareholders thought of this is not stated, but some sense of financial stringency appeared with an agreement to reduce the committee to seven members.

One of the assets claimed for the Brimpts sett was the ready availability of timber from the estate. It is surprising therefore to find that in 1854 in particular, Devon Tin bought quantities of timber in many varied sizes from the Buckland-in-the-Moor Estate[43]. Most of this was between March and October 1854 when the only development in progress was the sinking of the winze shaft. This was cut through hard ground and did not require support, but adaptation to the new engine shaft would have used timber. Larch, scotch, oak planks and a little ash were the woods purchased.

1855 started on a good note, with the sale of 23cwt of black tin for £48[44]. It was apparently the second parcel of ore to have been sold according to later reports, the first undated sale having raised about £15.

In January, two general meetings were held[45] which showed that the capital had dwindled to £446 11*s* 0*d* at the end of November 1854 and to £300 2*s* 8*d* at the year end. At this time, the winze, now called the new engine shaft (the only indication that Mr Perkes' ideas were being implemented), had reached the 26fm level and for 10fm below the 15 fm level had been sunk through good tin ground. The plan was now to stope the ground laid open with expectations of returns of tin in three months. The picture painted was a bright one, with a very good six-head stamping mill able to process 200 sacks per week ready to accept the ore raised. North Mine was at last moving from the development phase to production. It was agreed that development work be restricted to the engine shaft at North Mine and to driving the 26fm level.

On the subject of finance, it was decided to raise more funds by releasing reserved shares for purchase by the shareholders.

Quite what happened next is not recorded, but it is believed severe weather stopped operations for so long that the mine became flooded for in the next report from North Mine on March 5th[46], it says "the wheel went to work again on the 1st inst.. I expect by Wednesday the water will be in fork to the bottom of the shaft (26fm)".

On March 8th, Captain W. Thomas, superintendent, had set six men to stope the bottom of the 15fm west at £3 per fm, four men in the east at £7 per fm and four men to drive the level east at £7 per fm. These men had to pay for all drawing, filling and landing (i.e. subsequent handling of the mined ore). At this time the dressing floors at North Mine were still unprotected from the weather and the planned transfer of the "iron house" from South Mine is mentioned. This was possibly the movable building which had until recently served as a chapel and schoolroom at Brimpts[47].

On March 12th[48], James Thomas, manager of the mines (not to be confused with William), reports progress of 2ft in the eastern stopes, 3 ft in the western and 1 foot in the 15fm level.

On the 24th[49], it was 1 foot 1 inch in the eastern, 2fm in the western and 2ft in the level, raising 50 sacks to the surface. (If nothing else, these figures graphically illustrate how slow manual methods were.)

Then on the 26th March[50], everything was at a standstill again as renewed severe weather froze the leat again.

Work resumed so that by April 2nd[51], 2fm had been stoped in the east, 1fm 5ft in the western and 4ft 6in in the level, raising 100 sacks to the surface. We also get the first report of tribute working (payment by a share of the produce sold), the 15fm east being let to four men at £7 per fm and 12*s* in 20*s* for the tin.

On April 18th[52], the 15fm level had been driven 4ft. The stopes were now let on tribute, to five men in the pitch west of the engine shaft, to five men in the eastern pitch and to two men in the back of the 15fm west.

Captain James Thomas' next report on April 23rd was read to the shareholders meeting[53]. He confirmed that the pitches were let on tribute at an average of 13*s* in 20*s*, that the stamps were now operating and that he could prepare a parcel of tin for sale in a month or six weeks. This looked promising, but the finances certainly didn't. In January £76 16*s* 4*d* had been expended, only £20 13*s* 5*d* in February (time of the stoppage), then £100 10*s* 11*d* in March plus £5 to a Mr Reid, leaving just £97 12*s* 0*d*. No mention is made of receipts from the proposed share offer so this seems not to have been supported. An offer had been made (by a source not identified) to rent South Mine at £30 per annum plus one tenth of the produce. This seems derisory after all the investment, but after discussion, it was deemed acceptable. A call of 1*s* 6*d* per share was then made on the shareholders.

In *Mining Journal* for the 19th May[54], James Thomas reports the raising of 500 sacks of saving work in four weeks. 650 sacks had been stamped and 300 more were ready. The dressing was proceeding satisfactorily and "in the course of a few weeks, the ore will be ready for market". No hint there of any crisis, the mine swinging into full production despite the drain of capital. That however was the last report from the mines that we have been able to find. It is easy to conclude that Devon Tin simply ran out of funds, but it may be that closure was forced by another twist to the story. As mentioned earlier, Devon Tin's bankers were Strahan, Paul and Company which itself collapsed in June 1855 amidst allegations that it had unlawfully disposed of £22000 worth of securities on deposit[55]. Any funds received by Devon Tin as a result of the cash call would have been lost in this collapse as well as any residue of the original capital and the whole project brought to a halt, an ignominious end to the spirited venture.

References

Abbreviations used are:-

PRO Public Record Office

DRO Devon Record Office

DuCo Duchy of Cornwall

MJ *Mining Journal and Railway Gazette* (at Cornish Studies Library, Redruth.)

1. PRO E101/265/19. Information supplied by Dr Tom Greeves
2. PRO E101/266/21. Information supplied by Dr Tom Greeves
3. The Stannary of Tavistock, H.P.R. Finberg, 1949, *Report & Transactions of the Devonshire Association* **81**, 155-184
4. DRO 48/14/40/3 (original and transcript)
5. PRO PROB /11/24 Will of Sir John Shilston.
6. DRO 46/1/3/9
7. DRO Baptisms 1708, Widecombe-in-the-Moor Register. *The Devon and Cornwall Record Society*, 1938
8. DRO D564 M/F14 Volume 16, page 51
9. *MJ* 8th Sept. 1849, 436
10. DRO 924B/B2/1
11. DuCo London. Dartmoor Proceedings 1793-1800, 18th April 1799. Information supplied by Dr Tom Greeves
12. DuCo London. Mineral Grants Volume 1. Information supplied by Dr Tom Greeves
13. *MJ* 29th Sept. 1849, 466
14. *MJ* 23rd March 1850, 138
15. *MJ* 10th August 1850, 378
16. *MJ* 2nd Nov. 1850, 522
17. *MJ* 13th Sept. 1851, 442
18. *MJ* 17th July 1852, 347
19. DuCo London May 1852. Information supplied by Dr Tom Greeves
20. *MJ* 20th March 1852, 138
21. *MJ* 29th May 1852. 259
22. *MJ* 29th May 1852, 262
23. *MJ* 5th June 1852, 265
24. *MJ* 10th July 1852, 329
25. *MJ* 29th Jan. 1853, 70
26. *MJ* 12th March 1853, 145
27. *MJ* 21st May 1853, 305
28. *MJ* 4th June 1853, 332-333
29. *MJ* 25th June 1853, 382
30. *MJ* 9th July 1853, 414
31. *MJ* 16th July 1853, 429
32. *MJ* 1st Oct. 1853, 614
33. *MJ* 12th Nov. 1853, 708/9
34. *MJ* 26th Nov. 1853, 740
35. *MJ* 3rd Dec. 1853, 757
36. *Mines of Devon: North & East of Dartmoor*, A. K. Hamilton Jenkin, 1981, 112. (Published by Devon Library Services, a very useful but little known book still available on loan from Devon Libraries.)

37. *MJ* 31st Dec. 1853, 830
38. *MJ* 7th Jan. 1854, 6
39. *MJ* 21st Jan. 1854, 37
40. *MJ* 15th April 1854, 242
41. *MJ* 2nd Sept. 1854, 581 and 16th Sept. 1854, 618
42. *MJ* 7th Oct. 1854, 668
43. Buckland-in-the-Moor Estate timber sales ledger 1850-73, pers. comm. M. Brown
44. *MJ* 13th Jan. 1855, 24, 29
45. *MJ* 20th Jan. 1855, 37 and 3rd Feb. 1855, 66
46. *MJ* 10th March 1855
47. *Old Dartmoor Schools Remembered 1*, Mary Stanbrook, 1991, 73/4
48. *MJ* 17th March 1855, 166
49. *MJ* 24th March 1855, 182
50. *MJ* 31st March 1855, 198
51. *MJ* 7th April 1855, 214
52. *MJ* 21st April 1855, 246
53. *MJ* 28th April 1855, 260
54. *MJ* 19th May 1855, 309
55. *Trewman's Exeter Flying Post*, 28th June 1855, 7 (West Country Studies Library, Exeter.)

Surface Remains

Although there is no access to the underground workings and all buildings and machinery have been removed, there is still much of interest to be seen. A self-guided trail starts at Brimpts Farm and takes visitors around the three main sites, but for those with a deeper interest, a fuller description of all the sites now follows.

WARNING
Old mine workings are potentially dangerous sites. If you visit these mines, you must exercise due care and use common sense. Areas such as open shafts which offer obvious hazards have been fenced off, but there may be unrecorded shafts or unstable areas that could collapse without warning if walked upon. It is particularly advisable therefore that children are not allowed to play in the workings.

The Gully and the Dartmeet 'Mylls'

Workings stretch from (and under) Brimpts Farm eastwards down towards the East Dart River (see Fig. 8). The earliest activity may have been tin streaming followed by three phases of excavation; as Brymstebeme and Ester Brymstorbeme in the 16th and 17th centuries; as the 'shaft near the stables' in 1798-1807; and as the gully part of Old Brimpts and South Mine between 1848 and 1855.

In the flat ground between the bottom end of the gully and the East Dart River is an area either side of the stream which appears to have been excavated (bottom of Fig. 8). This is where, because of sudden slackening of the gradient, cassiterite eroded from the lodes and washed away would have settled. This area may therefore be a small early streamwork, but the evidence is inconclusive.

The most obvious part of the workings is the gully itself (SX 669738), a long, narrow rather pear-shaped excavation where, reportedly, two major lodes, called north and south, and a lesser one were worked from the surface downwards commencing in the early 16th century. At that time, it was not viable to mine hard granite with the tools available, but happily, chemical alterations during the mineralisation process and later surface weathering rendered the granite adjacent to the lodes much softer enabling removal of the ore down as far as the decomposed granite persisted or as far as water flowing into the workings permitted (in this case, the steep hillside enabled the openwork to drain down towards the river). The residual granite was sufficiently strong to maintain vertical sides to this excavation so giving the appearance of a long, deep quarry along the west-east line of the lodes. Today, the visual impact of the workings has been reduced by infilling of the deepest areas at the west end and along the south side with rubbish, but as a gauge to the original depth, this would have been about twice the distance to the top of the 1798 wheelpit which can be seen against the north wall of the gully. Looking at this later wheelpit carefully, it can be seen that it is sited in a gap between the north wall of the gully and a line of granite islands that the miners left undisturbed. We believe the channel in that gap has been left by the removal of ore from the north lode and that the much broader area between the islands and the south wall was originally where the south lode which dipped steeply to the south was intersected by a lesser north-dipping lode, such junctions being highly regarded by the miners as they contained rich tin deposits. The small channel diverging to the ESE from the narrowing east end of the gully may be the line of the intersecting small lode.

In early mining, an open excavation where the granite was thoroughly decomposed might have been worked by allowing water to wash away the lighter material leaving the tin (cassiterite) behind. There is a small stream flowing to the south of the gully which could have been diverted for this purpose, but if so, all trace has now been lost under Brimpts Farm. A leat could also have been brought from higher up the East Dart River and there are likely-looking banks running along the hillside north of the gully. We are satisfied however, that these originated as strip lynchets connected with early farming. One appears to have been used as a leat as far as Dolly's Cot, but a survey (by RCHME) showed the fall to run away from the gully, so this leat is not associated with the mining.

The ore may simply have been broken into small pieces and hand sorted at the gully before being taken to the knacking mill across the river. No trace of the mills has been found within the Badger's Holt walls, but the leat supplying the water can be traced from there almost to its start at the East Dart River. An apparent reservoir is alongside the top section of the leat. We can see no reason for a deliberate pool at this point and the depression may be natural, an abandoned river course, or man-made for some other purpose. Adjoining the Brimpts bank, what appears to be a small surviving portion of the headweir across the river can still be seen, especially when river levels are very low.

Of the 1798-1807 operations, the surface remains are fragmentary and the declaration of Richard Tuckett is the main documentary evidence, there being no known mine plan. The shaft mentioned is most likely to have been outside the present gully fencing, close to the top gate. No trace now remains, but it would have been in line with the long axis of the wheelpit in the north side of the gully since this was a waterwheel of up to 13ft (4m) diameter driving rods to power pumps in the shaft, the wheelpit site being unsuitable for stamps.

The declaration confirms that there were stamps and hence, another waterwheel and dressing floor, but the location of these is uncertain except that the phrase "down to the stumps" indicates they were lower than the Potatoe Field (plantation) workings. Two sites have both the gradient to suit the waterwheel and flat ground for the dressing floor, namely the areas at the top, west end of the gully and the bottom, east end. No evidence has been found at the upper end (although this could have been obliterated by later farming and farmyard developments), so we favour the lower site where there is some supporting evidence. Firstly, the tailrace from the pumps wheel is conducted down the gully in a leat channel along the presumed north lode. Where the gully narrows the course is lost due to collapse of the gully walls, tree falls and a later shaft, but the feasibility of a supply to the lower site is certain. Secondly, adjacent to and south of the deep adit entrance is a flat area. This is bounded on the west by a boundary wall across the small valley which, at its north end turns abruptly NE for a few metres, then NW for a couple of metres, then NE again to form a stout retaining wall against an elevated triangular platform bounded on the west side by spoil-covered high ground and on the NE by the discharge stream from the adit. The small stream from Brimpts Farm is conveyed under this site in a stone-capped culvert so clearly this area had a special function and the 1806 2in draft of the *Old Series* Ordnance Survey 1in maps shows a small enclosed structure. Unfortunately, the southern end of this flat area has been severely eroded by floodwaters and the northern part is buried under a rampant growth of nettles and brambles so no features are detectable without excavation. If this flat area was the dressing floor, there must have been a stamps wheelpit close by. Whilst the site certainly could house such a waterwheel, no trace of this has been found to date. The adit was cleared in later operations and the redundant wheelpit may have been demolished or covered up in the course of this.

Of the workings themselves, little is known. There was, as mentioned, a shaft at the west end and the deep adit whose entrance is in the cutting at the east end also dates from this time. A shallow gully SW of this entrance, which deepens towards the west then apparently stops, may be a blocked adit to workings on the south lode.

In the final phase of working, Brimpts Tin Mining Company cleared the deep adit from the entrance westwards. The adit entrance route can be seen, but the adit itself is blocked by debris, allowing passage only to water. A short distance to the west, at the start of the narrow neck of the gully, a small shaft was sunk, presumably for ventilation. A depression in the ground marks the site now and this should not be crossed. The deep adit passage almost reached under the *c*1798 wheelpit before turning south then west to pick up the south lode and follow it to the engine shaft. It is assumed that this was a clearance of the 1798-1807 shaft. At this time, clearance down to adit level only was attempted, so no pumping facilities were required. It was Devon Tin who subsequently developed the shaft as shown on their outline drawing Fig. 2, reproduced from the mine plan, with a flat-rod system coming in from the left (west), driving a bob-weight coupled to the pump rod in the shaft. The frame in the background supporting a conical attachment was a whim for hauling ore up the shaft, the illustration suggesting a simple man-powered capstan. All this was removed when the mines failed and the shaft was capped and forgotten. Some years ago, a loud roaring sound was investigated and it was found that the capping had suddenly collapsed. The cavity was subsequently filled in and levelled leaving no trace.

The Plantation

Dealing first with the workings (at SX 667739, see Fig. 9), the most obvious surface remains are the three cuttings joined end-to-end that form a less than straight line along the course of the roughly N - S

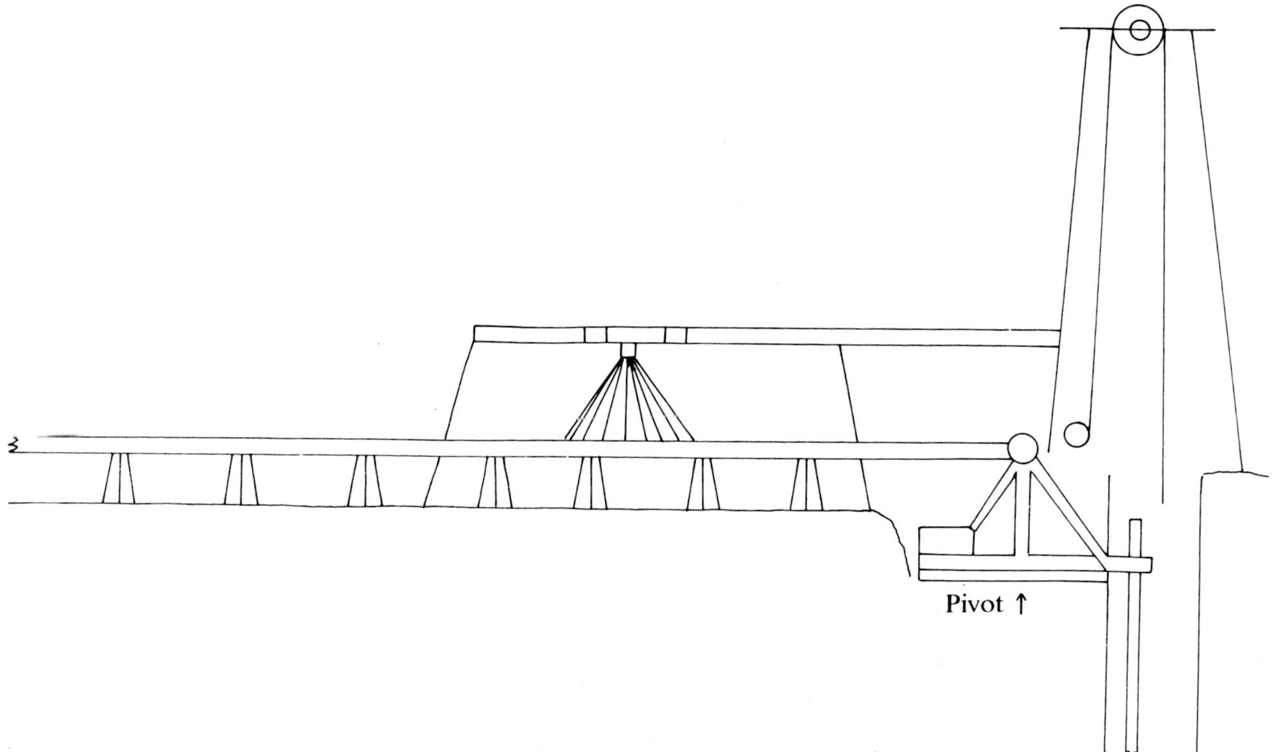

Fig. 2. Mine Plan Drawing of the Gully Headframe and Plant[1].

caunter lode. Although there is no specific documentary identification, we believe these originated as surface workings from probably the early 17th century. The subsoil here is clearly softer than in the gully, leading to the v-section required for stability.

In the 1798-1807 operations, a level was driven underground along the line of the lode. This had its adit entrance (now filled in) at the head of the lowest cutting.

In 1849, the adit was cleared and much of the ore produced by Brimpts Tin Mining Company was taken from here. In particular, a junction between the caunter plantation lode and a west-east lode supposed to be a continuation of one of the lower gully lodes was heavily worked. Strangely, there appears to have been no surface working of this W-E lode. This Company also started the shaft in the centre of the workings. As this was driven below adit and therefore drainage level, pumps were installed driven by a line of flat-rods from the waterwheel in the plantation. The shallow channel for these rods can be seen crossing the small rise to the west and there is a corresponding gap in the collapsed old boundary wall just SW of the shaft site. When Devon Tin took over, they abandoned the new shaft in favour of the gully below Brimpts. The pumps were removed and a triangular v-bob installed to turn the power of the flat-rod chain through about 55° down towards the gully engine shaft. The channel occupied by the flat-rod extension can be seen going downhill towards the small quarry outside the plantation, by which point it was being carried for the remainder of the route on stands above ground level. The plantation shaft is now fenced off as, at the time of writing, the conical depression marking its site was showing signs of imminent collapse of the shaft capping. The enclosure must not therefore be entered.

Following the line of the flat-rods towards the WSW, the processing area built in 1850 by the Brimpts Tin Mining Company is approached (see Fig. 3). This is centred around a large wheelpit which, being still open, is fenced off for safety. The pit is built of granite and housed a wheel claimed to have been 28ft diameter (8.5m) by 4ft breast (1.2m). At the easterly end of the pit, the water discharged into a tailrace culvert built partly of granite slabs and partly of natural bedrock. It took the water under the trackway along which ore was carried from

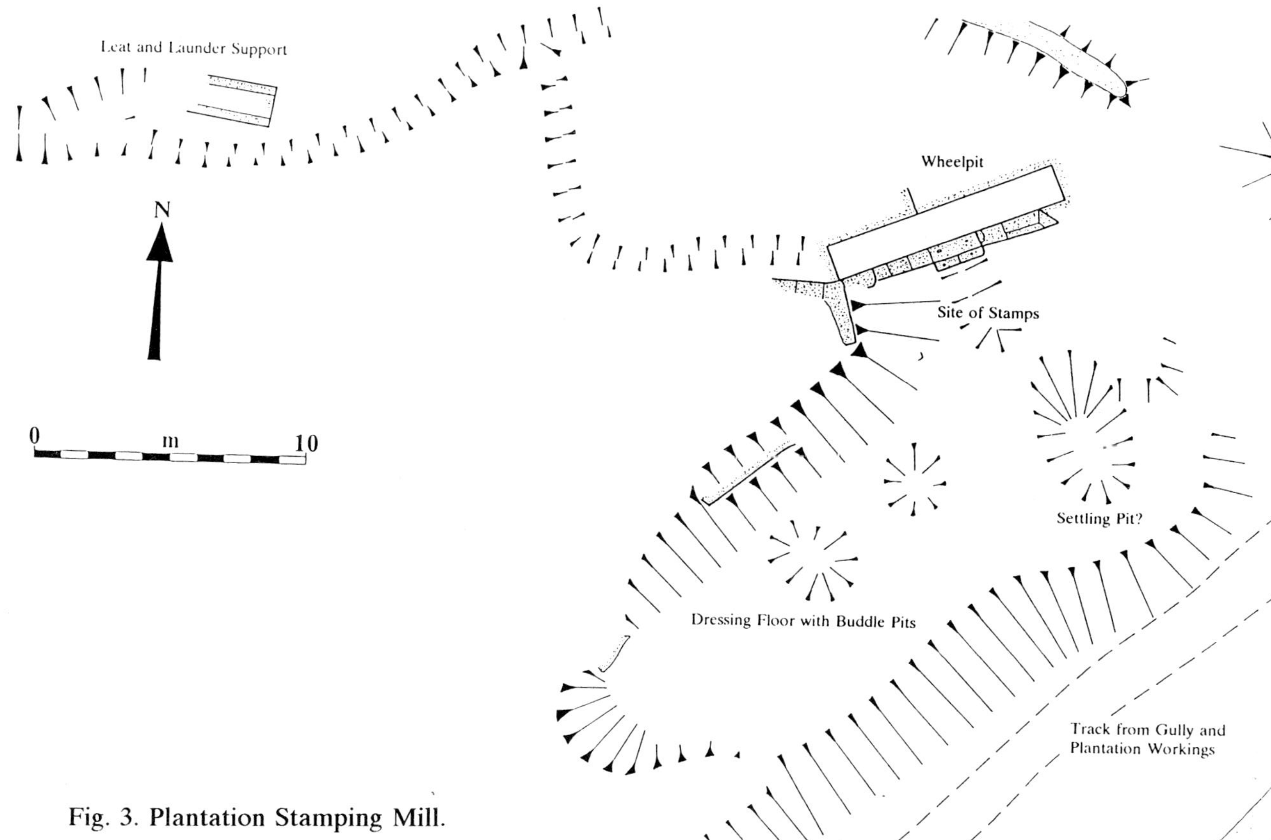

Fig. 3. Plantation Stamping Mill.

the gully and plantation workings to the stamps. These were sited in a 'house' at the long southerly side of the wheelpit. In the middle of this side is an outer, lower wall. The central axle of the waterwheel was coupled to the stamps axle by gearing and both this lower wall and the wheelpit wall have holes in their upper surfaces to secure the bearings for these.

Ore was probably fed from the top of the mound down a pass or feed chute into a line of six stamps at right angles to the wheel. The resultant slurry of water and pulverised ore flowed into a settling pit, probably the depression, originally lined, between the wire fence and the track below. Water flowing through this pit carried away the unprocessable fine slimes and the residue was periodically dug out and taken onto the dressing floor. This was to the SW of the wheelpit fenced enclosure on a level area excavated into the sloping hillside and having a retaining wall along its northerly side (part obscured by soil build-up). Two very shallow depressions mark the pits in which the buddles were built. Final processing would have been carried out in the wooden tubs called kieves on the continuing flat area beyond the buddles. (This dressing floor has not been uncovered to preserve it from damage. The North Mine upper dressing floor is very similar and the detail is much more obvious.)

If we now move from the dressing floor over the mound to the area NW of the wheelpit, the v-shaped leat channel can be seen approaching from the west and this leads to a rectangular drystone platform. Originally, a wooden launder on trestle supports would have carried the water horizontally from this platform to the top of the waterwheel, surplus water being directed by a hatch into the wheelpit. Small feed branches would also have supplied the stamps and the dressing floor.

On the northerly side of the waterwheel, the axle would have driven a crank to which the flat-rod chain was coupled for pumping water from the workings.

The Brimpts Mine Leat

Starting from just below the Higher Cherrybrook Bridge (at SX 634768 see Fig. 1, p5), the mine leat follows a twisting four mile route to Brimpts. Much of it is accessible to the public, but sections also cross private land and these should not be entered without prior permission.

The leat initially follows the Cherry Brook on its east side, passing through forestry plantations where the channel is still in use as part of the drainage system. On reaching Dunnabridge Common, it curves eastwards just above the 350m contour line, passing through various newtakes. Above Dunnabridge Pound, the leat is visible either side of the Dunnabridge-Bellever track (Postman's Road) but the channel itself has been completely obliterated by the later track. Near this point, the newer 1850 cut diverged from the original *c*1800 route and the old course can still be seen a few metres above the later cut as a shallow channel. The two routes continue, later diverging slowly, until beyond Huccaby Tor. In many places the old course is barely visible and easily confused with animal tracks.

Below North Mine, the leat was tapped to supply the waterwheel of the *c*1850 workings (described shortly). No obvious remains of the sluice are now visible, but close by is one of a dozen granite clapper bridges that provided crossing points over the leat. This one, where the ore from the mine was brought to the stamps, is a wide one, some others consist only of a single stone.

The route of the later leat was carefully chosen to pass just over the small dip behind Huccaby Tor and it is past here that original and later cuts reunite. The leat then passes back into Brimpts Newtake where, as it approaches the plantations, it splits into two separate routes. The left-hand one, curving away towards the NE, is the original route. It curves as it descends the hillside, then straightens and heads for the plantation boundary wall where all trace of it is now lost. We believe the original *c*1800 route was to the east along a slight valley, passing just northeast of the top of the plantation workings (then Potatoe Field), then dropping down the hillside to supply the gully pumps waterwheel. However, the careful observer will spot another leat which branches off the *c*1800 route just prior to its disappearance near the boundary wall in the newtake. This can be traced through the plantations, passing just west of the crossroads between the forestry road and the track from Brimpts Newtake towards Brake Plantation, to merge shortly with a stream that joins the East Dart at the northern limit of Brimpts Northern Wood. Originally, this leat may have flowed into another leat just NW of the crossroads, this latter originating in the mire in the Newtake, its continuing route now lost in the plantations. This part of the leat appears to post-date the mining.

Going back to the junction of *c*1800/1850 routes, the right-hand branch is the 1850 cut which heads for the SE corner of Brimpts Newtake then into the plantations. Dense tree cover makes it difficult to see, but it passes a few metres south of the visitor trail to follow the old eastern boundary of Snider Park Plantation, later turning abruptly to pass through this and head straight for the plantation waterwheel. Again, this route has a branch leat, in this case continuing down the boundary wall before diverging to run parallel to it, but a short distance inside the plantation. It emerges close to Brimpts' entrance gate where all further trace is lost. We can speculate on the function of this branch, but its true purpose is currently unknown.

North Mine

This is a large site, so we will start at the top with the mine itself (SX 653751, see Fig. 10) and then move down the valley towards the dressing floors. The mine has two known phases of working. Of the earlier phase we have no specific documentary record so can only date it from visual evidence as a 16th or 17th century openwork. (Many names of these early openworks have in fact survived, as lists in wills for example, but about half of these give no clues as to their original location.) The west-east lode has been worked by a sequence of pits and shallow gullies over a length of about 135m (450ft). To the west of this, trial pits at regular intervals in a line extending over the small ridge mark attempts to find further worthwhile tin deposits along the presumed continuation of the lode. To the east there are also trial pits, but these are rather more fan-shaped in distribution so the lode either vanished or split into several smaller veins in this area. Trial pits are also scattered down the valley towards and beyond the dressing floors. They may have been the initial pits used to locate the lode.

Extending down the valley from just west of the later engine shaft (fenced off) is another long channel which may mark early work on a small caunter lode, but later operations have made it impossible to establish this with certainty. The mine was therefore essentially a single lode working in an area where a north-south fault the later miners called the 'slide' crossed the lode. Such junctions are often more richly mineralised than the individual lodes and this probably accounts for the limited lateral extent of the workings here.

Within the engine shaft fenced enclosure, two shafts can be seen. The more easterly is a circular shaft which appears only to extend about 6m below the surface, apparently giving access to a shallow level. No mention of this is made in the *c*1850 reports and it was unknown until it suddenly opened up a few years ago. The arched passage visible between this and the engine shaft suggests it may be one of the original lode-back pits from perhaps the 17th century. Unfortunately, the exploration needed to establish this would be too dangerous.

Moving on to the *c*1850 operation and starting by the wall at the west end of the workings, the scant remains of the mine buildings can be seen as rectangular platforms with only the bottom part of the rear walls surviving as part of the boundary wall. Originally there was an office, a materials store, a blacksmiths and a carpenters' shop.

A circular pit on the line of the lode and on the buildings side of the Dunnabridge-Bellever track marks one of two adit shafts. This was an exploratory shaft dug down to 5fm which would have provided ventilation to the 5fm or adit level. In fact, the 5fm level is not recorded as having reached quite this far.

Crossing the track and heading towards the engine shaft, a large excavation, usually with a pond in the bottom, can be seen. This almost certainly was largely dug out after mining ceased, the material possibly being used to infill dangerous parts of the workings, but it would have been partially excavated prior to that as part of the early workings. At the western end, a v-shaped excavation, almost certainly part of these old lode workings, extends towards the track. This is shown on an 1886 O. S. map as the site of a rectangular 'building' and slight signs of foundations can be located. This structure was presumably sited deliberately to utilise the depth of the excavation beneath and, sited between carpenters' shop and engine shaft, with drainage down towards that shaft, it would have made an ideal and ready-excavated site for the saw-pit that was constructed in 1853 at the same time as the horse whim. The area between the wire fence and the pond was the site of this horse whim (see Fig. 4).

Immediately above the engine shaft enclosure is the slight circular platform about 9.5m diameter marking the site of the predecessor of the horse whim, almost certainly a manually operated capstan.

The engine shaft itself is basically rectangular, having been divided off to separate the footway from the haulage area. It would also have contained the pump rod connected at the top to a balance bob and then via flat-rods to the waterwheel in the valley below. The shallow excavation leading out of the fencing to the south would have been the bob pit.

Extending away to the south is the gully mentioned earlier as a possible early excavation on a caunter lode. This is also the site of the adit that connected with the 5fm level. Today, the adit entrance is completely infilled and the floor level about 3m below the ground level in the gully. Further down, just beyond the infilling by the stunted hawthorn tree, the level in the bottom of the gully is at adit level and undoubtedly the water pumped from the mine would have flowed through the adit and away down this channel to fan out over the plain below.

About 60m east of the engine shaft is a large depression with the second adit shaft in the bottom. This did connect with the 5fm level and during Devon Tin's development of the mine, a winze (a shaft driven down from a level) was sunk from the 5fm to the 15fm level and down to 26fm. This was drained by a six inch pump driven by an extension to the flat-rods with presumably a pump rod connecting to the winze via the adit shaft. Because the best ore was at this eastern end, this adit shaft/winze combination was converted to become the New Engine Shaft in name, but there is no record of the installation of any surface equipment. It might be assumed that the large depression here was a consequence of the new shaft development, but the mine plan shows it pre-dates the winze and may have been a particularly rich spot in the old workings.

Moving down the valley towards the dressing floors, two features are of interest. Firstly, the flat-rod system route, which originally comprised a series of rods linked in a long chain kept permanently under tension.

Fig. 4. Mine Plan Drawing of North Mine Horse Whim and Headframe[2].

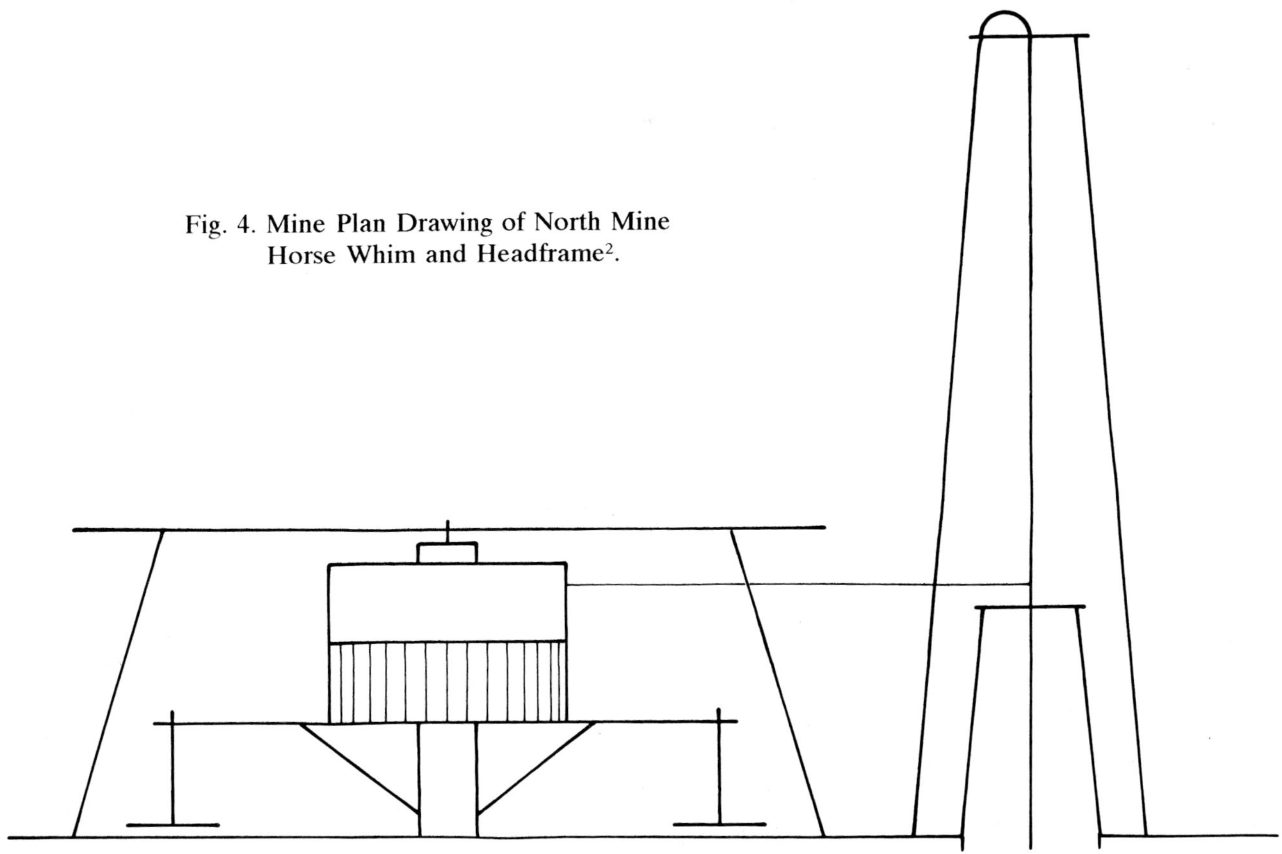

This chain was kept just above ground level over the top half of its route, probably on roller guides, but the low siting of the waterwheel and a slight rise in the ground meant that part of the lower route was in a shallow channel which can still be seen. The second feature is a track that connected the adit and the stamps. The mine plan shows a large spoil heap in the channel leading from the adit and this seems to have been part removed or spread out to fill the small gully adjacent to the small hawthorn tree. This created a loading area from which a track runs initially westwards then curves and heads for the dressing floor, crossing the leat by the clapper bridge before swinging round and up onto the platform above the stamps. A few metres SW of the hawthorn at the track top, a pair of ramps back-to-back can be found. These originally carried the track over the flat-rods' route, the rods running in a narrow channel between the ramps, a short overgrown section of which can still be found. The rest of the track in this area is difficult to spot, but nearer the lower end, a raised carriageway with a shallow ditch either side can be seen, largely because of vegetation differences between it and the surrounding rough grazing.

Following this track over the leat and up onto the stamps loading platform gives a view over the remainder of the site (see Fig. 5). Looking southwards, the site is divided into two by the wheelpit just southeast of the platform and its long tailrace channel. Both are now largely infilled, the former with stones from the stamps area and the wheelpit itself, the latter with peat, so although this wheel was only slightly smaller than the plantation waterwheel, the impact is far less dramatic.

The shallow channel east of this platform would have contained the flat-rods connected to the east side of the wheel and also the launder bringing water from the leat to the wheel, to the stamps and to the upper dressing floor. The six head of stamps would have stood on the flat area bounded to the north by the platform, to the west by a low retaining wall and to the east by the wheelpit, the coupling to the wheel being by gearing.

To the south of this area, adjacent to the tailrace, can be found a shallow rectangular pit with a second less well-defined pit leading in turn from its south end. These, we believe, were the stamps settling pits where the slurry of pulverised ore and water from the stamps was

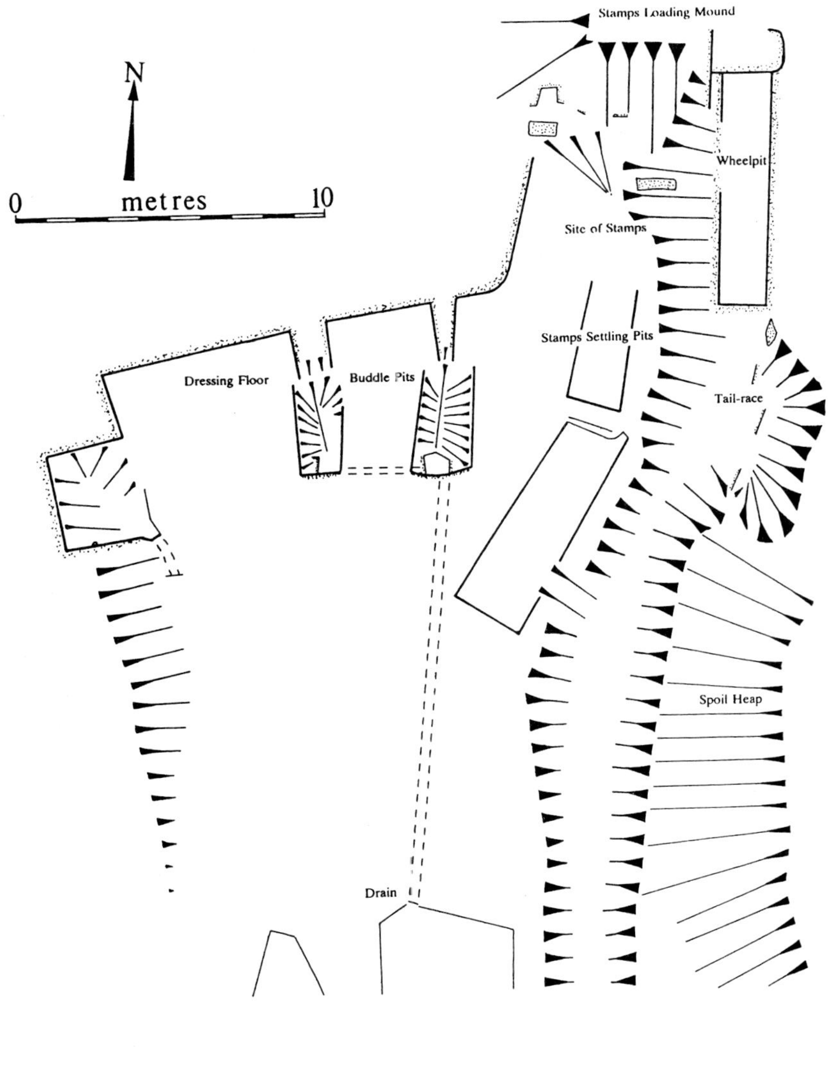

Fig. 5. North Mine Stamping Mill.

allowed to separate, the heavy ore settling in the first pit whilst the lighter slimes and water carried on into the second, the water there either soaking into the ground or spilling down into the tailrace. Periodically, the ore would have been dug out and transferred to the dressing floor, the flat area to the west surrounded on two sides by a small retaining wall.

The dressing floor contains two well-preserved pits in which the rectangular buddles were sited. Two piers jutting from the retaining wall probably supported the upper ends of the buddles and their water supply launder, whilst at the bottom (south) ends of the pits can be seen the drains which conveyed the water and tailings waste not into the tailrace as might be supposed, but southwards through a stone-lined drain to empty out onto a flat area where the water and waste would have been separated. Whether this is all there ever was is uncertain. If a tailings lagoon existed, then its outline is no longer clear.

To the west of the buddle pits is a flat area and beyond it again, an area recessed into the retaining wall with a sloping floor leading to a drain. Taken in isolation, these two areas would have been where final processing in the wooden tubs or kieves took place. In this case however, we shall see that there was a lower dressing floor, the function of which is uncertain so some processing may have been split between the two floors. Before leaving this area, it is worth mentioning that just west of where the buddle drains empty onto the plain, there is a bottle-shaped pit which looks as though it should have been a waste lagoon for water from the kieves area, but we have found no evidence of a connection and the function of this pit is therefore uncertain.

On the east side of the tailrace channel, the most prominent feature is a long spoil heap containing waste from the tailrace excavation. Features a little east of this are prehistoric and unconnected with the mine, but east of the lower end of the tailrace channel there is a rectangular floor area bounded by retaining walls or partial walls on three sides which appears to have been a lower dressing floor. Now this is a strange place to choose since it is quite remote from the other facilities, but the crucial clue as to reason is the small leat which leaves the tailrace channel and crosses the upper retaining wall about a third of the way along. We know that Devon Tin suffered serious water shortages and by using waste water for this lower dressing floor, the situation was eased. The floor area itself is largely featureless apart from a slight depression near the eastern end which may have housed a buddle and we cannot therefore judge what proportion of the processing was carried out here relative to the upper floor, but evidence that it was a dressing floor is provided both by the leat and the drainage channel along the southern edge, now partly collapsed. The floor may have held the flat tables called frames to process ore too finely crushed to be separated in the upper buddles. The drainage channels lead into a stone-lined culvert under the apparent path leading south from the centre of the floor edge. This culvert appears to end some distance from the floor without detectable connection to a large rectangular shallow pit nearby which seems likely to have been a tailings lagoon as at the upper floor.

Winford Newtake Adit

About midway along Winford Newtake (the enclosure bordering the East Dart River south of Laughter Hole House) a shallow channel littered with stones of quartz and quartz-tourmaline descends towards the East Dart. At the foot of the scarp is a fairly well hidden adit (SX 663754). If we take the shallow channel as marking the course of an eroded vein, then the adit seems to have been an exploratory working to assess the mineral value. Starting in from the river bank, there is an overgrown spoil heap beneath an approach channel which continues until deep enough for the adit passage to be cut through solid rock. The adit entrance is half blocked by fallen debris which holds back about a 1m depth of water in the adit mouth. Exploration has shown that the passage is only 22m long, with a 5m spur passage following a 150mm wide vein containing what appears to be a friable mixture of haematite with finely ground tourmaline and quartz.

It is thought that this is the working referred to during the *c*1850 operations as the East Dart River lode. The adit itself may have been started by the Brimpts Tin Mining Co. or it may date back to around the *c*1800 period, but we found no evidence to suggest an earlier date. The local legend that it connects with North Mine is certainly untrue.

Other Workings

There are two minor surface workings within Brimpts Newtake at about SX 660731 and SX 661734 where short lengths of west-east lodes have been exploited by a series of pits. Nothing is recorded, but they most probably date to before 1800.

Other Sites Investigated

A short distance to the Brimpts side of Dunnabridge Pound in a spot currently obscured by gorse growth, is the old Brownberry dipping well. In *High Dartmoor*, Hemery suggested that the passage excavated through the growan behind the cistern is a former adit. Our exploration found nothing to support this view.

In the corner of Snider Park Plantation closest to Huccaby Cottage is a structure closely resembling an adit, there being an opening under a large boulder with an approach channel cut through the sloping ground which connects to an apparent drainage channel down towards Huccaby Cottage. Investigation has shown however that the 'adit' has only been excavated for a very short distance and it is more likely that this is where a spring has been followed back to its source and then piped underground as a (former) water supply for Huccaby Cottage.

References

1. Devon Record Office 4672A/HS/R282C Abandoned Mine Plan R282C; Devon Tin; South Mine, February 1854.

2. Also R282C, Working Plan of the Devon Tin Mines, undated, but the state of development suggests it was the one mentioned in Nov. 1853 as prepared by Mr Gulley of Tavistock.

Small Finds

Since its failure, the mining plant of this sett has been comprehensively cleared so that few artefacts have been found. Those that have survived all appear to date from the 1848-1855 period.

1. Fragment of cast iron found adjacent to North Mine engine shaft.

Part of a cylinder of wall thickness 38-40mm and having an internal diameter of about 175mm (7in), this 50mm x 80mm fragment with scoring on the inner surface in a direction along the axis of the cylinder was probably part of the barrel of the pump which was recorded as of 6in diameter.

2. Iron wedge.

Found at the eastern end of the plantation wheelpit, this wedge, now a lump of rust, was about 60mm broad by 12mm deep at the thick end, 97mm long, and 50mm broad at the sharp edge. Its use could have been to secure a part of the machinery or for stone splitting.

3, 4. A short, round iron bar and a tapered piece of iron respectively, found together on a ledge inside Winford Newtake adit.

The bar, originally of iron but now oxidised and covered with a concretion of rust and small stones, was of nominal 25mm diameter and about 300mm long. Its probable use was for drilling holes in the granite whilst driving the adit.

The tapered piece is even more heavily covered with concretions but is almost 240mm long having a cross-section of about 25mm by 20mm at one end and about 20mm by 10mm near the other end, the actual end rather rounded. The tapered bar is slightly curved along its larger side and may be part of a miners' pick broken off and put to use as a wedge for forcing off pieces of rock during driving of the adit.

5. Piece of flat wooden board originally with metal fastening, from Winford Newtake adit.

Although very soft, constant wetting has preserved the basic shape of this piece, presenting an outline resembling a paddle with a rather pointed broad end and an M-shaped narrower end with signs of where a handle or similar fitting may once have been attached. Whilst

Fig.6. Piece of Wooden Planking.

there is a possibility that this object may have been introduced to the adit after the mining, if contemporary, it may have been originally a paddle used to stir the contents of a kieve, but which broke and was put to some temporary use in the adit. The board is 680mm by 150mm at the widest part. The thickness at the point originally protected by the fastener or fitting is 30mm, the remainder of the surfaces having been eroded by the rotting (see Fig. 6).

6. Piece of slate.

A piece of slate believed to have come from the sluice in the leat at North Mine stamping mill was presented to Plymouth City Museum some years ago. We have no detailed information on this item.

Details of these artefacts and all other features of the mining sett have been recorded in the Devon County Sites and Monuments Register at County Hall, Exeter. Anybody wishing to conduct further research on the site should be able to view the entries by appointment. The control record reference is SX67SE/14.

Notes on Mineralisation, Processing and Viability

Mineralisation

The general picture of the origin of Dartmoor is well established, the granite pluton having been intruded into Devonian and Carboniferous strata beneath a mountain chain about 280 million years ago and subsequently exposed by erosion. The processes that resulted in the mineralisation as the granite cooled have been less well understood. Hydrothermal activity is now accepted as the overall driving mechanism with hot aqueous saline solutions circulating through the granite in fissures and microfractures under high pressure, the chemicals in the solutions reacting not only internally but also with the surrounding granite to produce the mineral deposits, the greisens, the tourmaline and the kaolinisation.

Until recently, the mineral deposits were thought to have derived from one process, crystallizing out in sequence in order of solubility to give zones or shells outwards from the centre of the pluton with tin ore first, then copper and so on. However, the current belief, as described by Dr Richard Scrivener[1], is that this is a major oversimplification, there being not only more than one contemporaneous process such as differentiation into tourmaline and greisen forms, but also a series of stages and events separated in time. Fortunately in our case, the cassiterite deposits in the north of Dartmoor are considered to have resulted from a single simple intrusive event during the main-stage mineralisation about 277 Ma ago.

It appears that as the granite cooled, a pocket of high density, high salinity boron-rich fluid was trapped between the carapace of solid granite and the molten magma below. As fractures developed in the carapace, the fluid escaped, sometimes with explosive violence, depositing initially tourmaline (a boron rich cyclosilicate) and quartz (silicon dioxide) in the veins; then later, these two plus cassiterite (tin dioxide). As time progressed and cooling continued, repeated reopenings of the veins resulted in new deposits containing chlorite (a complex silicate of sheet-like form) and quartz, followed shortly by specular haematite (an iron oxide) and finally quartz alone. So this represents an assemblage of oxides quite separate from the sulphides associated with the copper, lead, zinc etc. found around the granite and it came from the interior of the granite not scavenged from surrounding sediments. At least it came from the interior prior to deposition, but black tourmaline is not considered a magmatic substance and the boron needed to form it may have been captured from fresh marine sediments as the granite rose through them, which in turn makes it less certain that the cassiterite originated within the granite. Clearly, as our understanding has advanced, so also has been revealed the complexity of the processes and we await further research findings with interest.

At Brimpts, we have no access to the lodes and even spoil heaps are minimal so it is difficult to build a representative picture of the deposits. The trend of the main lodes is west-east and at all three main sites there are junctions with north-south veins, the latter being the dominant working in the plantation. This trend is shared with other mines in the area, but not with the rich Birch Tor/Vitifer complex with its NE-SW main lodes, a difference that needs further investigation.

In terms of minerals, all findings at Brimpts have been consistent with the oxide assemblage described above, sulphides being absent. Tourmaline, quartz and red-brown haematite are common to all the mines, but so far, only one tiny sample of specular haematite has been observed, near North Mine, a contrast with the areas to the northeast where it was a common and unwelcome impurity. Chlorite can be found easily at North Mine, but is much less obvious in the gully or plantation and this may have some significance because the miners described the North Mine lode as being of a different nature. Stones containing up to 40% cassiterite were reportedly found in the workings, but these would obviously have been sent for crushing and we certainly have not found any more despite looking hard! The average tin content reported of about 1-3% is unlikely to be obvious in a hand specimen.

Processing

The lack of impurities in the Brimpts ore enabled the miners to use a very simple processing sequence to extract and concentrate the black tin. In fact, despite the passing of three centuries since the engravings in Fig. 7 from Agricola's *De Re Metallica*[2], the wet stamping apparatus at the top and the buddle at the bottom would

Fig. 7. Wet Stamping Mill and Buddles, *De Re Metallica*, Agricola, 1556.

have changed very little. They did the job very well, but were labour intensive and some other mines were starting to introduce the more efficient round buddle at about this time. Photographs of both rectangular and round buddles can be found in *Tin Mines and Miners of Dartmoor* by Tom Greeves.

The lodes were narrower than the space needed to work them, so both lode and some wall rock would have had to be mined. This would have been hand sorted at the mine, only the 'saving stuff' being transported down to the stamps, the remainder being dumped in the workings if possible.

At that time, the large Cornish stamps were used, six vertically set heavy wooden lifters with cast iron heads each raised by teeth projecting from the rotating drive axle, the axletree or turnbarrel, and allowed to fall repeatedly onto the stones. Wet stamping would certainly have been used. The stones would have been fed in with water, as this was not only, literally, a flow process (unlike the batch handling of the much earlier dry stamping), but the water removed the small particles as soon as they formed. This prevented them from being further crushed or abraded and thereby reduced the amount of unprocessable very fine slimes produced and the consequent loss of the cassiterite in them. It was important though to reduce the ore to the size of sand grains since the cassiterite was finely dispersed through the rock and to liberate a substantial proportion of this, the ore had to be crushed down to a size at least as small as the individual crystals. Total liberation could not be achieved so the output always consisted of a mixture of particles of waste, cassiterite and part waste/part cassiterite.

In passing into the settling pits, the heavier particles would have tended to settle out quickly, the waste further along whilst the slimes were washed straight through. Whether this separation was made use of is not known.

Once settled, the crushed ore would have been dug out and fed into a rectangular buddle. The ore was mixed with water and introduced at the top end of an inclined flat-bottomed trough and, essentially, the denser cassiterite settled out in a band at the top (the heads), whilst the waste (the tailings) continued to the lower part. The process is more complex than it appears so the cassiterite/waste divide was not precise leading to a mixed zone of middle heads or middles. The skill of the tin dresser lay in his ability to divide off the tailings and dump them, to further concentrate the heads and to extract as much cassiterite as economically possible from the middles. These fractions may therefore have been passed through the buddles in different combinations several times and even restamped if necessary.

The next processing stage was in wooden tubs called kieves where the concentrate was added steadily to some water and stirred until a dense slurry in suspension was achieved. The stirring then stopped and the kieve was repeatedly hit with a bar causing the cassiterite to pack tightly in the kieve bottom with the impure material above and water at the top. This was poured off and the impure concentrate on top scraped off for further processing whilst the finished black tin concentrate below was dried and prepared for sale.

The processing in kieves seems to have been a means of overcoming a drawback of the buddles. These were excellent for separating the dense cassiterite from lighter waste, but far less effective where cassiterite particles were mixed with denser waste such as particles of part cassiterite, part tourmaline so that the solids had similar densities much higher than that of the water. By stirring in a kieve until the concentrate was in suspension in a dense slurry, each particle would effectively be in a medium of average density close to its own and would tend to move upwards or downwards according to slight density differences, a process then accentuated by beating the kieve with a bar in a manner analagous to a method known as jigging.

The finished product would not then be pure cassiterite, but a mixture of this plus waste plus undesirable contaminants. Parcels of tin put up for sale from different mines would therefore be assessed individually and priced accordingly so both the ore content and the dresser's skill could affect the mine's profitability.

Viability

It is easy to say with hindsight that had Devon Tin not wasted so much of its capital on South Mine development, it would have been able to support North Mine into full production, but even so, could this have been profitable? With the limited figures available, we can only assess this in broad terms, but over the final year to the end of March 1855, the capital had dwindled at an average weekly rate of £25.70. This was basically for North Mine only with little development so if we add sufficient to pay a dividend of 5% on the £4000 capital plus an allowance of £300 per annum for additional capital expenditure such as the new wheel, then a target figure for the mine to earn of £35 per week is reasonable. This equates to almost one ton of black tin to be sold per week.

Now, North Mine had six head of stamps able, we are told, to process 200 sacks per week each of 1¼cwt. This gives 250cwt maximum throughput of ore from which to produce 17cwt of black tin concentrate or 8½cwt per 100 sacks. Typical figures in the reports from the mine mention yields per 100 sacks of as little as 1cwt or, from the winze, an average of 2 to 2½cwt, with a high of 5-7cwts in one early estimate, so unless the 'good tin ground' in the winze below the 15fm level was exceptional, it is improbable that the average could even have been reached let alone maintained.

The Brimpts set-up was low volume, high labour cost. It needed to be just the opposite, high volume, low cost. This could have been achieved, as Mr Perkes pointed out, with the processing, but even with the use of explosives it is doubtful whether the ore could have been mined from veins 600mm or less in width in sufficiently high volume at low enough cost to be really profitable. Had this latter been achieved, then a further real problem appears since the lateral extent of the deposit along the single lode was quite small. Future prospects therefore depended on ore reserves at depth and indications such as the absence of workable lodes from the more heavily eroded north central Dartmoor area suggest the lodes in these peripheral zones were quite shallow, certainly nothing like as extensive as some Cornish deposits, so the available ore would probably have become exhausted very quickly. Sadly, Brimpts, like very many other mines on the High Moor was not the good investment the manifesto made it out to be. The insurmountable problem was that there was no way in which the reserves of ore at depth could be assessed by looking at the lode at the surface. It was necessary to sink shafts and drive levels with all the capital expenditure that entailed in order to sample the lode, so Brimpts really should be regarded as a large trial exploration.

Investment in a new mine was therefore an absolute lottery and the knowledgeable adventurers accepted that there would be many more failures than successes, but without these mine trials, the worthwhile lodes could not be found - nothing ventured, nothing gained! On the other hand, the earlier streamworks and shallow openworks where development was minimal could be, and probably were, worked profitably. So, despite the inglorious end, Brimpts may well have been a worthwhile tinworking site.

References

1. British Geological Survey, Exeter on University of Exeter DCAE Course D95B011EXC.

2. *De Re Metallica*, G. Agricola, Hoover translation, 1950, Dover Publications Inc..

Glossary

ADIT. A tunnel cut into the hillside and sloping down towards the entrance to provide drainage at that level and for workings above. When pumping was available, water from deeper levels of a mine would typically only be raised to adit level and then discharged along it. Also used as an access.

BLACK TIN. To distinguish concentrated tin ore from tin metal in documents or speech, the ore was called black tin after the very dark brown to black appearance of large cassiterite crystals. Crushed dry cassiterite usually has a pinkish-brown colour resembling drinking chocolate.

BOB, V-BOB, BOB-PIT. A bob is a device for transmitting mechanical power using a pivoted beam rocking in a to-and-fro motion as in the beam of a beam engine. Bobs were also used with weights on one end to counterbalance a load such as the pump-rods in a shaft. In this case, an additional beam at right angles to the first could be added to enable the power of a line of flat-rods to be turned through 90° to operate the pump-rods (see Fig. 2, p35). For convenience, this bob was often sited in a pit, the bob-pit, at the shaft head. Where a line of flat-rods needed to be redirected through an angle, the beam could be formed as a V of appropriate angle with the pivot at the junction of the arms. This was called a v-bob, angle-bob or turn-bob.

BUDDLE. A shallowly inclined plane at the top of which a slurry of water and crushed ore was gradually introduced allowing the dense mineral to settle in a band near the top of the slope whilst the lighter waste was washed further down. Initially, the buddle was in a rectangular pit, but from about 1850 a round form was introduced, the feed being at the centre of a shallow, conical slope.

CROSS-CUT. A passage or level cut at about right angles to the line of the main lode.

CROSS-COURSE. A vein, probably non-mineralised running at about right angles to the main lode.

DRESSING FLOOR. The area where crushed rock was purified into a concentrate by separation from waste rock.

ENGINE SHAFT. Usually the principal shaft of a small mine, engine in this sense meaning having machinery for pumping.

FLAT-RODS. A series of wooden or metal rods pivoted at the ends and connected in a long chain to transmit power in a to-and-fro movement from a waterwheel or steam engine generally to pumps in shafts. Such a chain can only operate effectively if kept in tension during both power and return strokes.

FORK, FORKING-WATER. A term used to describe the pumping of water from a shaft.

KNACKING MILLS. Ore crushing mills, where rock was pulverised by the repeated dropping of iron-capped heavy vertical wooden beams, were initially called knacking or knocking mills (knack = sharp blow or sound). This name later changed to stamping mill.

LAUNDER. A wooden trough on supports and carrying water, an aqueduct.

LEVEL. A horizontal passage in a mine providing access to the lode(s) and connections to shafts, adits etc..

OPENWORK. The general term for shallow excavations from the surface along the line of a lode to produce a quarry-like cutting.

SETT. Each mining site had a recorded set of bounds around its periphery, the area within being known as the sett.

SHAFT. The general term for an essentially vertical passage from the surface to a level or levels underground, but also engine shaft as above; adit shaft, a shaft from the surface to a level which is connected to an adit; and winze shaft, an underground shaft - see *winze*.

STOPE, STOPING. The action of mining the ore from the lode was called stoping and the area excavated the stope.

STREAMING. The working of alluvial cassiterite deposits usually in valley bottoms by hand removal of stones followed by use of a stream of water to wash away soil and waste to leave the cassiterite behind.

STUFF. Ore mined from the lode and sorted ready for processing.

TURN-BARREL. One name for the axle driving the stamps lifters and fitted with teeth (cams, tappets) to lift each head two or more times per revolution.

WHIM. The general name for the hoisting equipment raising ore and lowering timbers etc. down a shaft.

WINZE. An essentially vertical passage as per a shaft, but commenced from an underground level and excavated in a downwards direction. A similar excavation in an upwards direction would have been a raise or rise.

Bibliography

Agricola, G. 1556 *De Re Metallica* Translation by Hoover, H. C. & L. H. 1950 Dover Publications, Inc. (New York)

Atkinson, M., Burt, R. & Waite, P. 1978 *Dartmoor Mines - The Mines of the Granite Mass* Exeter Industrial Archaeology Group

Burt, R., Waite, P. & Burnley, R. 1984 *Devon and Somerset Mines - Metalliferous and Associated Minerals 1845-1913* University of Exeter in association with Northern Mines Research Group

Collins, J. H. 1912 *Observations on the West of England Mining Region* Royal Geological Society of Cornwall

Dines, H. G. 1956 *The Metalliferous Mining Region of South-West England* HMSO Reprinted by British Geological Survey 1988 with addenda and corrigenda

Finberg, H. P. R. 1949 The Stannary of Tavistock *Report and Transactions of the Devonshire Association* **81**

Greeves, T. 1986 *Tin Mines and Miners of Dartmoor - A Photographic Record* Devon Books

——— 1985 The Dartmoor Tin Industry - Some Aspects of its Field Remains *Devon Archaeology No. 3*. Devon Archaeological Society

Hemery, E. 1983 *High Dartmoor - Land and People* Robert Hale Ltd.

Jenkin, A. K. Hamilton 1974 *Mines of Devon Volume 1: The Southern Area* David & Charles

——— 1981 *Mines of Devon; North & East of Dartmoor* Devon Library Services

Lysons, Rev. D. & S. 1822 *Magna Britannia Volume the Sixth, containing Devonshire* Thomas Cadell

Stanbrook, M. 1991 *Old Dartmoor Schools Remembered 1* Quay Publications (Brixham)